WHEN GOD IS GONE
EVERYTHING IS HOLY

In these times, to be devoted to contemplation is to carry all you love in the vessel of yourself into uncharted terrains, sustained by ineffable astonishment as you are asked to surrender, bit by bit, so much of what you carry in that vessel. Readers on the contemplative journey will find that Chet Raymo leads them to the point where contemplation must align itself with the revelations and demands of an unfolding universe; the only adequate context for choosing a "seamless garment of being."

Miriam Therese MacGillis, O.P.
Founder/Director of Genesis Farm, Blairstown, New Jersey

Chet Raymo is one of the best science writers working today, and in this remarkably thoughtful and balanced book he has confronted the realities of the physical world that science has given us as only a truly spiritual person could: with courage and integrity, awe and wonder. His personal journey from committed Catholic to scientific agnostic resonates deeply because he addresses the questions that all thoughtful people face. Regardless of which path you choose to take, it is the journey itself that really matters, not the destination, and I can think of no one more qualified than Chet Raymo to be your guide.

Michael Shermer,
Publisher of *Skeptic* magazine and
monthly columnist for *Scientific American*

WHEN GOD IS GONE
EVERYTHING IS HOLY

The Making of a Religious Naturalist

CHET RAYMO

SORIN BOOKS Notre Dame, Indiana

---

www.sorinbooks.com

ISBN-10 1-933495-13-8 ISBN-13 978-1-933495-13-2

Cover and text design by Katherine Robinson Coleman.

Cover image © Superstock Inc.

Printed and bound in the United States of America.

Library of Congress Cataloging-in-Publication Data

    Raymo, Chet.
    When God is gone everything is holy : the making of a religious naturalist / Chet Raymo.
        p. cm.
    Includes bibliographical references.
    ISBN-13: 978-1-933495-13-2 (hardcover)
    ISBN-10: 1-933495-13-8 (hardcover)
    1. Raymo, Chet. 2. Religious biography. I. Title.
    BL73.R39A3 2008
    211'.7092—dc22

    [B]

                               2008012734

contents

acknowledgments

It has been a long strange journey, and I have been helped by many people along the way. Here are a few who gave shape to my religious life.

My mother Margaret and father Chester. Sister Jane Frances Beck and Sister Dominica Gobel of the Nashville Dominicans, two brilliant women who were my teachers at Notre Dame High School in Chattanooga in the early 1950s. The many fine men of the Congregation of Holy Cross whom I encountered at the University of Notre Dame and Stonehill College; I would particularly note Tom Lockary, Robert Kruse, and Bartley MacPhaidin. Other friends who guided me: Frank Ryan, David McCarthy, Peter Lucchesi, Nancy Carrigg, Tom Clark, Robert Goulet, Maurice Sheehy, John Holstead, Stephanie Holstead, Philip Naughton, and Barbara Naughton. Chris and Jennie Kettel and Jane Dunn provided me with a lovely place to write. I especially thank Bob Hamma and the other good folks at Ave Maria Press for making a beautiful book. My children Maureen, Dan, Margaret, and Tom helped keep me on the crooked and wide. My wife Maureen has been at my side for a half-century of the journey, always ready to puncture any balloons I inflated with hot air. Thanks, Mo.

The first chapter on Mr. Blue is adapted from an essay that appeared in *Spritus: A Journal of Christian Spirituality*, and is used with permission. A few other parts of this book are adapted from essays that appeared in *Notre Dame Magazine*; thanks to the editors for inviting me to write and for permission to adapt the material.

vii

chapter one

Mr. Blue Redux: An Introduction

Sometime during my sophomore year at the University of Notre Dame in 1955–56, my girlfriend (now my wife) gave me a copy of Myles Connolly's novella, *Mr. Blue*. "You'll like this book," she said, "the main character reminds me of you." Her appeal to my ego was too much to resist. I read the book and wondered what I had in common with the hero, the eponymous Mr. Blue.

Connolly was a Jesuit-educated graduate of Boston College and on his way to becoming a successful Hollywood screenwriter when he published *Mr. Blue* in 1928. The book immediately achieved a cult status, inspiring several generations of young Catholics to find more in their faith than formulaic prayers and rote dogma. The hero of Connolly's story, known only as J. Blue, is a passionate Christian, living hand-to-mouth in New York City in the service of Lady Poverty and his fellow men. He flies brightly-colored kites and releases gay balloons from the top of a skyscraper, where he lives in a cheerfully-decorated packing crate and entices a brass band to make music under the stars. He celebrates life with outgoing gusto, then prostrates himself in solitude before the crucifix.

Blue is a modern St. Francis, a Manhattan saint. He has no doubts that he was put on Earth for a purpose, and that the purpose is to live his life as a work of Christian art. He has no interest in women and, curiously, seems oblivious to official liturgies of the Church. By contrast, when the book came into my hands, I was a rather stolid engineering student from Chattanooga, with little on my mind except making good grades and chasing after young women. I had, of course, heard of St. Francis, but I couldn't have told you within three hundred years when he lived. Or why he had been sainted.

But my future wife knew me better than I knew myself, because something about *Mr. Blue* immediately resonated in my spirit. It was a time of lively reinvention in Catholic higher education, of abounding confidence and intellectual religiosity, all of which made me receptive to Blue's exhortation to live a joyously muscular Catholicism and to bear Christ's cross gladly, if and when it came. Blue is above all a man of faith. He is skeptical of philosophy, of books even. The enemy of faith is "scientific agnosticism," which Blue accounts as the pernicious and spiritually-deadening philosophy of our times. One cannot counter scientific agnosticism with reason and argument, he believes. The only answer to the prevailing spiritual malaise is a life lived with passionate, unquestioning Christian conviction.

If there is one bit of dialogue in the novella that moved me profoundly, it is Blue's answer to the narrator's question, "Isn't the golden mean the secret of something or other?" "Yes," replies Blue, "mediocrity." That was the challenge of the book: not to live life meanly, to avoid compromise. I resolved to follow in Blue's footsteps. If I was going to live as a Catholic, I would do so without reservation. I put pebbles in my shoes, sand in my bed, and did the Stations of the Cross at night on bare knees along a cinder path. I spent hours in prayer at Notre Dame's replica of the Lourdes grotto. I read George Bernanos, Leon Bloy, Francois Mauriac, and Graham Greene, devoured Thomas Merton's *Seven Storey Mountain*, and briefly flirted with becoming a Trappist monk. I drove my future wife crazy with my violent swings between hormone-driven sexuality and guilt-ridden asceticism. By the time I came back to Notre Dame as a married graduate student in 1960, I was planning to go to San Salvador or Bangladesh in the service of the Church. And, like Blue, I flew kites. Whatever life would bring, I was determined it would not be mediocre.

That was nearly half-a-century ago.

I reread *Mr. Blue* recently. Again it was my wife who put the book into my hands (she found it in the middle-school library where she worked a volunteer). She wondered, I suppose, what I would make of it, after all these years. My first impression was surprise that I could ever have been inspired by a book that is so slight, so trite, so without literary merit. Connolly was no Georges Bernanos, no Graham Greene. His book is a compendium of platitudes, and his character Blue now seems an insufferable prig who thought most of his fellow human beings had as little capacity for life as cabbages. However, the book is probably a pretty fair reflection of the place I was in the late 1950s and early 1960s, in the throes of my newly-energized Catholicism. My faith, like Blue's, was simplistic, and I too was something of a prig. I was utterly confident I possessed the Truth.

In retrospect I can see that it was a supercilious dogmatism, not charity, that caused me to volunteer for the foreign missions, in spite of the fact that by then I was the father of a very young child. The Church wisely resisted this undertaking; to bring our infant daughter to San Salvador or Bangladesh would have been irresponsible, and besides, my wife's enthusiasm for the venture was never the equal of mine. I settled down to the study of science, got a PhD in physics, went into teaching, and eventually became the scientific agnostic so disparaged by Blue. The point of religion, I now believe, is to celebrate the unfathomable mystery of creation; my work as a teacher and writer has been to discover glimmers of the Absolute in every particular, and to praise what I find. I did not end up serving Lady Poverty, but then neither did I worship Mammon. Most fundamentally, I have given up the certainty that I know the Truth. I no longer believe that Christians are any closer to God than right-living people of any other faith. Faith no longer matters to me so much as attention, wonder, celebration, praise. I have sought to maintain something of Blue's childlike capacity to be astonished, his wide-eyed conviction that everything is shot through with grandeur. A kite is a kind of prayer. So is a brass band.

And the golden mean? Is it the secret of something or other? Oh, yes. It is the secret of life—my life, at least. There is something to be said for moderation, especially in a world wracked by religious strife, and by the hypocrisy and arrogance of institutional churches. The golden mean is the secret of tolerance, of modesty, of a healthy skepticism—of knowing that every dogmatic definition of God is a pale intimation of the truth and, inevitably it seems, an excuse for jihad, pogrom, or crusade. Mr. Blue, for all of the tolerance he wears on his sleeve, is something of a zealot, and I've arrived at a place somewhere between passivity and zealotry. I've had my fill of "muscular" Christianity, of creeds, and of doctrines of infallibility. Call it, if you wish, mediocrity; I happily embrace the epithet.

This book tracks a half-century journey from traditional, faith-based Catholicism to scientific agnosticism, a journey that began at the University of Notre Dame in the 1950s and ended in the breathtaking twenty-first-century universe of galaxies and DNA. If you ask me if a scientific agnostic can be a Roman Catholic, I would have to answer no—at least not as the Church presently defines itself; there is no room in scientific agnosticism for the age-old distinctions between natural and supernatural, body and soul, matter and spirit that are so firmly affixed to Catholic orthodoxy. But there is a parallel Catholic tradition of ancient lineage, generally dismissed as heretical, but dear to the hearts of many Catholics, which emphasizes God's immanence and creation-based spirituality. "Saints" of that parallel Church, from Meister Eckhart to Gerard Manley Hopkins to Teilhard de Chardin, have been my companions on a journey to what can only be called, in all honesty, Catholic agnosticism.

chapter two

Like Shining from Shook Foil

F ew poets are as universally loved as Gerard Manley Hopkins, the gentle Jesuit priest whose verses brim with a conflicted reverence for nature and the divine. If ever there was a person caught between natural and supernatural, matter and spirit, body and soul, it was Hopkins. During his lifetime, his poems were known only to a few close friends; the first published collection did not appear until twenty-nine years after his death. Today, his verse is of particular interest to those of us who are committed to naturalism, but who—because we have been steeped in Catholic tradition—long for some glimpse of the Absolute.

He was born in 1844 into a moderately high-church Anglican family, but was drawn, seemingly irresistibly, to an ever greater degree of ritualism and asceticism. As a

7

student at Oxford he became a high-church Anglican then converted to Roman Catholicism and became a Jesuit priest—to the consternation of family and friends. Psychologists and literary biographers have tried to explain the trajectory of Hopkins's life, which led to an early death at age forty-five. It is commonly assumed that he hoped to subdue homoerotic feelings in a life of order and obedience. Whatever the case, there is a tension in his life and poetry between outer and inner sources of spirituality that may go far to explain our fascination with the man and his verse.

Even as a child, Hopkins had a passion for the natural world: plants, animals, hills, dales, streams, slants of light, the forms of frost, starry nights, comets, stones, bells, the aurora borealis, human faces. The felling of a tree could bring him to tears. His biographer Robert Bernard Martin tells of the time an old lay brother at the Jesuit seminary came upon Hopkins crouched in a path staring raptly at wet sand. Something about the glint of light on quartz grains compelled the young seminarian's attention. "Ay, a strange young man," said the brother later. "A fair natural 'e seemed to us, that Mr. 'Opkins."

A "fair natural," indeed. Hopkins's attention to nature had an intensity that can only be described as mystical. "What you look hard at seems to look hard at you," he remarked. He was attuned to a certain *inner-ness* of things, what he called "inscape." His sensitivity to this hidden essence of nature is manifest in his poetry:

As kingfishers catch fire, dragonflies draw flame;
     As tumbled over rim in roundy wells
       Stones ring; like each tucked string tells, each hung bell's
Bow swung finds tongue to fling out broad its name. . . .

Hopkins could not rid himself of the notion that by attending to the sensual world of *particular* things he was being drawn away from the spiritual and universal. Beauty, he imagined, is the enemy of sanctity. He sometimes practiced what the Jesuits called "custody of the eyes," forcing himself to walk though the world with his vision fixed at his feet. If he could not have the inscape of things, he would not settle for surfaces.

Or so he told himself. He was wrestling with an age-old dilemma that continues to bedevil us today: God's immanence versus God's transcendence. According to Martin, Hopkins found a way to resolve the dilemma in the writings of the medieval philosopher Duns Scotus, who taught that the material world was a sacramental symbol of God, not something separate from him. Although Scotus's theology smacks of pantheism—and was frowned upon by Hopkins's Jesuit superiors—it was an extension of the Christian doctrine of the Incarnation to include the phenomenal world that was such an important, if troublesome, part of Hopkins's spiritual life.

This melding of inner and outer worlds came to fruition in the wonderful sonnets of his last years that so move us today, such as "God's Grandeur," which begins with these lines:

> The world is charged with the grandeur of God.
> It will flame out, like shining from shook foil. . . .

Here, it seems, is a formula that lends itself as well as any to the religious naturalist's reconciliation of science and spirit. Science seeks the *universals* that order and animate the world. Spirit dwells on the inscape of *particular* things, the "shining." Call it pantheism, call it panentheism, call it a Scotean sacramental Incarnation; it doesn't really matter. In Hopkins's view, it is *there*—in whatever it is that charges the world with grandeur—that we encounter "the dearest freshness deep down things."

> The world is charged with the grandeur of God.
> It will flame out, like shining from shook foil;
> It gathers to a greatness, like the ooze of oil

Crushed. Why do men then now not reck his rod?
Generations have trod, have trod, have trod;
    And all is seared with trade; bleared, smeared, with toil;
    And wears man's smudge and shares man's smell:
        the soil
Is bare now, nor can foot feel, being shod.
And for all this, nature is never spent;
    There lives the dearest freshness deep down things;
And though the last lights off the black West went
    Oh, morning, at the brown brink eastward, springs—
Because the Holy Ghost over the bent
    World broods with warm breast and with ah!
        bright wings.

How he loved the natural world! I think of a line from
another poet, Mary Oliver: "I am sensual in order to be spiritual." That was Hopkins. He loved the sensual, but feared it
as a distraction from God. The Jesuits, to whom he gave his
short life, believed the senses were the enemy of sanctity,
that beauty was the Devil's share. The young men at the
Jesuit novitiate—eighteen, nineteen, twenty years old, at
the peak of their sexual and sensual awakening—were kept
occupied every waking hour of the day lest their idle senses
become an occasion of sin. They were even given "modesty
powder" for their bath to make the water opaque; God forbid
that they might be aroused to lascivious thoughts by the
sight of their own genitals. Hopkins seems to have borne
such training gracefully, and it must be said the Jesuit regimen was not at odds with his own ascetic inclinations.
When the years of novitiate were over and he embarked
upon his priestly duties, his Jesuit confreres seemed to have
understood that Hopkins was special in a spiritually sensi-
tive and conflicted way, and treated him with a certain pride
and tenderness.

We know from his writings that Hopkins was a constant
and perceptive observer of the night sky. He had just

enough astronomical knowledge to know what he was looking at, but not so much as to overwhelm his childlike sense of wonder. Once he noticed a faint blur of light in the constellation Cancer and thought it might be a comet. For three nights he watched it before deciding that it was a fixed nebula, not a comet. It was, in fact, a cluster of individually invisible stars, known to the ancients as the Beehive but at that time unfamiliar to him. If you have ever seen the Beehive—a faint smudge of light on the inky windowpane of night—you will know that it is not something likely to be seen by a casual observer.

Of Comet Coggia in 1874, Hopkins wrote in his journal: "I have seen it at bedtime in the west, with head to the ground, white, a soft, well-shaped tail, not big: I felt a certain awe and instress, a feeling of strangeness, flight (it hangs like a shuttlecock at the height, before it falls). . . ." The image of the feathered badminton birdie hanging momentarily motionless at the apex of its arc will resonate with any experienced comet watcher. But how many of us upon seeing a comet in the sky will feel to the same extent what Hopkins called "instress," that inexpressible awareness of an abiding mystery (the inscape of the thing) that lies hidden in every perception, and which sometimes reveals itself with a particular luminosity, "like shining from shook foil."

As a science writer, I am generally reluctant to use such phrases as "inexpressible awareness" or "particular luminosity" for fear of drifting into a kind of New Agey mysticism. What draws me to Hopkins, however, is the way his fiercely *exact* metaphorical language keeps his spiritual experience anchored in careful observation—as in these lines penned upon seeing Comet Tempel in 1864:

—I am like a slip of comet,
Scarce worth discovery, in some corner seen
Bridging the slender difference of two stars,
Come out of space, or suddenly engender'd
By heady elements, for no man knows:

But when she sights the sun she grows and sizes
And spins her skirts out, while her central star
Shakes its cocooning mists; and so she comes
To fields of light; millions of travelling rays
Pierce her; she hangs upon the flame-cased sun,
And sucks the light as full as Gideon's fleece:
But then her tether calls her; she falls off,
And as she dwindles shreds her smock of gold
Amidst the sistering planets, till she comes
To single Saturn, last and solitary;
And then goes out into the cavernous dark.
So I go out: my little sweet is done:
I have drawn heat from this contagious sun:
To not ungentle death now forth I run.

Each image here—from "spins out her skirts" to the gravitational "tether"—is grounded in science. (But what of Saturn,
which Hopkins calls "last and solitary"? Weren't Uranus and
Neptune known in Hopkins's time? Yes, but these verses
were written as a speech in a play set in the Renaissance,
when Saturn was indeed the outermost planet known.
Hopkins clearly knew his astronomy.)

There is something else going on here, something more
than merely metaphorical. We must imagine Hopkins in the
warm, dark morning hours of late summer of 1864. He has
woken early, restless, unable to sleep, trying to keep his
thoughts upon his prayers (he is presently a student at
Balliol College, Oxford, on vacation in North Wales), but
finding his attention pulled this way and that by the distract-
ing enticements of the night, including—yes, there, high in
the east between Taurus and Auriga, that slip of light, the
comet, spinning out her skirts.

Custody of the eyes! How hard he tried. How hard—to
keep the rich seductions of sight and smell and taste and
touch and sound from filling his thoughts to overbrimming,
from displacing that absolute emptiness that he was taught
to prepare for God to fill. How sad his sense of failure, his

worn-out early death, his soul wounded by struggle. He had hoped to see God face-to-face, unentangled in flesh—what Catholics call the Beatific Vision—and what he found instead was a Heraclitean fire, burning, burning, ever changing, all-consuming.

Cloud-puffball, torn tufts, tossed pillows | flaunt forth, then
    chevy on an air—
Built thoroughfare: heaven-roysterers, in gay gangs | they
    throng; they glitter in marches.
Down roughcast, down dazzling whitewash, | wherever an
    elm arches,
Shrivelights and shadowtackle in long | lashes lace, lance,
    and pair.
Delightfully the bright wind boisterous | ropes, wrestles,
    beats earth bare
Of yestertempest's creases; in pool and rutpeel parches
Squandering ooze to squeezed | dough, crust, dust; stanches,
    starches
Squandroned masks and manmarks | treadmire toil there
Footfreted in it. Million-fueled | nature's bonfire burns on.

Here, in these extravagant opening lines from a late poem, Hopkins is seemingly out of control, his so-called "sprung" verse springing about like a jackrabbit, his soul afire in the apprehension of a roiling skyscape—tumbling clouds, light, and shadow. He is near the end of his short life (he died of typhoid fever, weakened by several years of poor health). And although we might conclude that in this pell-mell poem—"That Nature is a Heraclitean Fire"—he has let language run amok, it is probably also true that his perception of the natural world had become so acute, so *soul-searing*, that he struggled to find a way for language to contain it.

Hopkins was certainly aware of the glittering successes of nineteenth-century science, but he did not have access,

say, to the overarching grandeur of Charles Darwin's evolutionary view of life. For him the Heraclitean fire burned
helter-skelter, catch-as-catch-can. But Gerard Manley
Hopkins, the tormented believer, and Charles Darwin, the
tormented agnostic, were not so far apart. They were both
creatures of the portal between knowledge and mystery
where the questing human spirit defines itself and endures.

Hopkins, like Darwin and every other questing scientist,
lived in the world of particulars but sought the universal.
Look! *These grains of glistening sand in the path. These tendrils
twisting at the top of the vine. These particles moving helter-
skelter under the microscope.* Poet and scientists devoting
their lives to the thing they perceived behind nature's veil,
the inscape, the general, the universal. Hopkins sought the
divine source of nature's beauty *as seen through a glass darkly*, the *Deus absconditus* of the mystics. The scientist is less
likely to anthropomorphize the hidden ordering principles
of nature, but seeks no less the inscape of things. Those of
us who count ourselves Catholic agnostics follow in the footsteps of Gerard Manley Hopkins, threading our cautious
way between the particular and the universal, tempering
our imaginations with scientific empiricism, but delighting
always in the eternal tease of nature's partially lifted veil.

chapter three

Ancient Mother of the World

A coy coquette. She stands on a pedestal in the Musee d'Orsay in Paris, the goddess Isis, lifting her veil to reveal a glimpse of bared breasts, a demure smile, an aura of mystery. What secret knowledge is hidden here? Approach, if you dare.

This sculpture—*Nature Unveiling Herself to Science*—was created by Louis Barrias in 1899. It gives expression to one of the oldest and most enduring themes in philosophy. Sometime in the early fifth century B.C., the Greek philosopher Heraclitus famously said "Nature loves to hide," and the history of Western philosophy can be taken as one long riff on the meaning of his words. What the goddess reveals as she lifts her veil is what Gerard Manley Hopkins called the inscape of things. The Renaissance astronomer

15

Johannes Kepler called it the *facultas formatrix*—a "forma-
tive capacity" that gives form and meaning to the universe.
The modern physicist seeks a few mathematical "laws of
nature" that apply across the universe.

For the religious person, the *facultas formatrix* is God,
and the idea of a hidden God is common in many religious
traditions. Certain Christian mystics spoke of the *Deus
absconditus*, the absconded divinity, or alternately, a "cloud
of unknowing." Call it as you wish—inscape, *Deus absconditus*, or *facultas formatrix*; the names are incidental. The mystic and the scientist have this in common: they seek the
same deeply hidden essence of creation, and both are, by
and large, content that much of what they seek remains
unknown. Mystic and scientist live at the portal between
knowledge and mystery.

Let me confess my own leanings at once: *Nature is partially, tentatively knowable, and natural science is our best bet
yet for obtaining reliable knowledge of the world.* Like most scientists, I don't claim Truth with a capital T, but I am convinced that the manifest successes of science are a sure sign
we are doing something right. I think of such discoveries
during my lifetime like the residual radiation of the big
bang, the drift of continents across the globe, and the dou-
ble-helix structure of DNA, discoveries that have revolution-
ized our understanding of the world. What revelation and
magic failed to achieve across many millennia of practice,
science, through its handmaiden technology, has realized in
mere centuries. But science doesn't deplete the mystery;
rather, the more we understand about the universe, the
more we are faced with an ever-deeper encounter with the
thing seen only through a glass darkly—the inscape, the
absconded God who hides in a cloud of unknowing.

Meanwhile, there she stands, on her pedestal in the
Musee d'Orsay, taunting our curiosity—the bared breasts,
the glimpse of toes—still, after millennia of scientific discovery, wrapped in mystery. She does indeed love to hide, this

enigmatic goddess who provoked Heraclitus, and I suspect that another two-and-a-half millennia from now we'll still be wondering what she has yet to reveal. The agnostic is her acolyte.

This is a book about living in the portal between knowledge and mystery, between the commonplace and the divine. "What makes the desert beautiful is that somewhere it hides a well," said Antoine de Saint-Exupery's Little Prince. We live in a universe that is vast and seemingly indifferent—a desert, if you will, of ultimate meaning. It is also a universe of hidden wells. But before we go in search of hidden wells, allow me to take a few pages to describe my personal journey from true belief to skepticism, not because I think my journey is in any way exceptional, but precisely because it is typical of Catholic agnostics.

I grew up in the 1940s and 1950s in the Bible-thumping southern United States, where every other telephone pole along the two-lane blacktops bore a sign that said, "Jesus is Coming Soon" or "Prepare to Meet Thy Maker." My family was Roman Catholic, a relative rarity in Tennessee. But I was raised to "be prepared." Armageddon may not have been just around the corner, as my Protestant evangelical neighbors insisted, but an eternity of happiness or torment was riding on my state of grace. I lived in fear that I might accidentally die with a mortal sin on my soul—some sexual peccadillo perhaps. ("Bless me, Father, for I have sinned. I had impure thoughts seven times. . . .") Sheep on the right, goats on the left. Fire and brimstone for the goats. Nothing exceptional about any of that; it was part of the spiritual landscape.

But I had parents who read books and loved ideas. A few exceptional high school teachers—Dominican nuns—taught me to value the life of the mind. By a stroke of good luck I went off to the University of Notre Dame in Indiana just as a new young president, Reverend Theodore Hesburgh, decided a Catholic university could also be a great institution of empirical learning. It was surely not the outcome that Father Hesburgh envisioned, but by the time I left Notre Dame after eight years of undergraduate and graduate education in science, I was well on my way to becoming a "lapsed" Catholic.

For that, I give Notre Dame credit. My teachers taught me to think for myself and gave me an education in science that made no reference to religion. The science I learned at Notre Dame was the same science that was taught at University of California at Los Angeles, where I also spent a few years of graduate training—or for that matter, at the universities of Tokyo, New Delhi, or Moscow. In science I was introduced to a way of knowing that transcends accidents of birth.

Married and with a fresh PhD in physics, I moved with my growing family to the New England of Emerson and Thoreau. By that time, I had pretty much worked through my Mr. Blue phase and had become a skeptic of sorts, willing to examine the verities of my cultural tradition. I had set out to live as a Thoreauvian *sojourner*. I did not want to be good because I feared hellfire, but because *it is good to be good*—good for oneself, good for one's family, good for one's fellow humans, good for the planet.

I no longer believed in the personal, transcendent God of my forebears, yet I still felt religious, was still enamored of the Catholic sacramental tradition. I had no time for miracles or the supernatural. But the more I learned about the natural world the more I stood in awe of its "inscape." I longed to give praise and thanksgiving. And to pray. "I don't know exactly what a prayer is," says Mary Oliver in a poem, "I do know how to pay attention." I paid attention. With others of a scientific temperament, I read the Book of Nature. Now, in the eighth decade of my life, I am cautiously willing to use the G-word for the mystery I found there, and unembarrassed to use the word "prayer" for attending with reverence to what I see.

The militantly atheistic biologist Richard Dawkins, whom I admire for many things, thinks it's a sham for someone of agnostic temperament to use the language of traditional religion. The word "God," for example. Or "prayer." These words have meanings defined by ancient usage, he says. "God," as almost universally understood, is a transcendent personal being who hears and answers prayers and intervenes miraculously in the world. To use the G-word as a stand-in for "inscape" or "Mystery" is to lend credence to an idolatrous anthropomorphism.

But there is something called natural religion (or, if you prefer, religious naturalism) that hides behind and within traditional faiths, and I am not so ready as Dawkins to surrender a venerable and evocative language of praise to traditional theists. I will continue to pray, if by prayer you understand me to mean attention to the world. ("Prayer is the contemplation of the facts of life from the highest point of view," wrote Emerson; "It is the soliloquy of a beholding and jubilant soul.") And I will try to live—as my Roman Catholic teachers urged me to live—in a state of grace. Not supernatural grace, to be sure, but the myriad natural graces that bless and hallow the everyday.

The religious naturalist foregoes a personal God. God defined *in our own image.* God invested with human qualities: justice, love, will, desire, jealousy, artifice, and so on— in short, the attributes of human personhood. To the agnostic, a personal God is the ultimate idolatry.

In his *Spiritual Exercises*, the Greek novelist Nikos Kazantzakis writes:

> We have seen the highest circle of spiraling powers. We have named this circle God. We might have given it any other name we wished: Abyss, Mystery, Absolute Darkness, Absolute Light, Matter, Spirit, Ultimate Hope,

Ultimate Despair, Silence. But we have named it God because only this name, for primordial reasons, can stir the heart profoundly. And this deeply felt emotion is indispensable if we are to touch, body with body, the dread essence beyond logic.

I have often quoted this passage in my various writings because it seems to capture profoundly the Deus abscondi-tus of the mystics, the thing seen through a glass darkly, the mysterium tremendum et fascinans of the theologian Rudolph Otto, the numinous flame that burns in every atom, every flower, every grain of sand, every star—the hidden thing behind nature's veil. Can Dawkins be right and Kazantzakis wrong? Is "God" the wrong word for the "dread essence beyond logic"? Give Dawkins this: the word is indeed almost irretrievably burdened with personhood. It is our golden calf, our idol.

Child psychologists, such as the Swiss scholar Jean Piaget, tell us that children instinctively give animate, personal characteristics to inanimate objects—draw a face on the sun, for example. Anthropologists tell us that all prescientific people are animistic in their religious beliefs, investing every tree, brook, and celestial body with personhood. What could be more natural? What metaphor is more ready at hand than the thing we know best: our self. For all of its grandeur and refinement, the idea of a transcendent personal deity who acts in the world is only the final manifestation of a primitive animism. A divine *Person* is not the Heraclitean mystery seen through a glass darkly, but a reflection of one's self in a mirror brightly. At the very least we should use the G-word with circumspection.

Still, for all of my agnosticism, I call myself a Catholic. Not because I can recite the Creed (I can't), or because I practice that particular faith (I don't), but because the substance of Catholicism went into my system like mother's milk. None of us can be free entirely from the cultural influences that shaped our ways of thinking and experiencing the world. Nor would I want to if I could. I cosset in my heart an unquenchable affection for Catholic tradition.

I am repelled, of course, by the triumphalism, paternalism, and authoritarianism of the Church, its Jansenism, supernaturalism, miracle-mongering, and misogyny. But the sacramental tradition is a treasured part of my being. A sacrament is a "visible sign of invisible grace," according to the Church, and "invisible" need not imply "supernatural." I experience every aspect of the natural world as the "visible" manifestation of an "inscape" that is deep and mysterious beyond my knowing. A hundred years ago, who could have imagined the dervish dance of the DNA or the ripples in the energy of the big bang that gave rise to galaxies. Who today can imagine what we will know a hundred years hence. The world is shot through with a grandeur that now and again flames out "like shining from shook foil." In Catholic tradition, one must be predisposed to grace to receive it. I wait. Alert. Always. For the shining.

I love the Catholic liturgical tradition—the wax, water, fire, chrism, candlelight, bread, wine, palm fronds, colors, chants, bells—the whole sensual celebration of the material world. I love the Campbellesque, sun-centered cycle of the liturgical year, and the canonical hours of the day. I love the monastic tradition of life lived with a balance of physical labor, intellectual study, and prayer, the last of which I would define—with Thomas Merton—as a quiet listening of the heart or, more simply, attention. I love the tradition of creation spirituality, heretical to be sure, but in love with the world and suspicious of dualities—Columbanus, John Scotus Eriugena, Meister Eckhart, Mechthild of Magdeburg, Julian of Norwich, Nicholas of Cusa, Giordano Bruno, Gerard Manley Hopkins, Teilhard de Chardin, and all the rest. I love the whole smoky, sexy physicality of Catholicism that inspired the art of Gislebertus, Gian Lorenzo Bernini, and Sigrid Undset, that sent Heloise and Abelard careening into mad abandon and smote Clare and Francis. I love the quintessentially Catholic dark night of the soul as much as I love the luminous Easter symbolism that goes with a planet tipped cockeyed on its axis.

Can I have all of that and still eschew the shabby panoply of miracles and the supernatural—what the poet Philip Larkin called the "vast, moth-eaten musical brocade" of traditional faith?

I am Roman Catholic by birth and upbringing, and also by immersion in the so-called Catholic Renaissance of the mid-twentieth century, a time of intensely creative Catholic art, literature, and philosophy. We devoured the likes of Thomas Merton, Teilhard de Chardin, Etienne Gilson, and Jacques Maritain. Once you have walked the walk with Georges Bernanos's country priest or Sigrid Undset's Kristin Lavransdatter (we will meet them later), you are marked for-ever with a sense of the sacramental. With them, I still attend with all my heart to nature's visible signs of invisible grace.

So this is my Credo. I am an atheist, if by God one means a transcendent Person who acts willfully within the cre-ation. I am an agnostic in that I believe our knowledge of "what is" is partial and tentative—a tiny flickering flame in the overwhelming shadows of our ignorance. I am a panthe-ist in that I believe empirical knowledge of the sensate world is the surest revelation of whatever is worth being called divine. I am a Catholic by accident of birth.

"In the beginning, there was not coldness and darkness: There was the *fire*," wrote the Jesuit anthropologist Teilhard de Chardin in *The Mass on the World*. He added: "The flame has lit up the whole world from within . . . from the inmost core of the tiniest atom to the mighty sweep of the most uni-versal laws of being."

It has been forty-five years since I first read those words. I was then a graduate student in physics, discovering a world of matter, energy, and natural law, and struggling to accommodate my new learning to the Roman Catholic faith of my youth. Teilhard de Chardin came into my life like a blaze of light. Here was a man, a Catholic priest no less, who sang the wonders of matter and energy, who turned the evolution of the universe into a theology of praise. I was not alone in my admiration for the lanky, enchanting Jesuit; many of my generation were caught in his spell. We were hungry for a way to reconcile science and spirit. Teilhard offered a vision of a world shot through with mystery and meaning—an animating fire that could only be perceived with the *scientifically-informed* eye of faith. He was, like his Jesuit confrere Gerard Manley Hopkins, an acolyte of the hidden God.

Then, in 1965, only a few years after Teilhard's works became available in English, and as I began my career as a teacher of science, physicists discovered the cosmic microwave background radiation, the all-pervasive afterglow of the big bang. Until that moment, most physicists believed in the so-called "steady state" universe, a universe that had always existed pretty much as we find it now. Beginnings and endings were anathema to physicists of the mid-twentieth century; they smacked of special creation, of divinity. But with the discovery of the cosmic microwave background radiation, the steady state universe was no longer tenable. In its place, we were offered a cosmos that began as a speck of superhot fire exploding outward. Every aspect of the universe we inhabit today, from quarks to quasars, was implicit in the big bang beginning.

It was a wild, beautiful story—creation as a singular, blazing fire—and Teilhard had seemed to anticipate it. It was the sixties, after all, a time of revolution and renewal, and suddenly science and faith were on the same track. Or so I

believed, as a young Catholic scientist hungering for spiritual wholeness.

From a perspective of forty-five years on it is clear that
what we found in Teilhard had very little to do with science.
He was a research anthropologist who made some exciting
fossil discoveries in China, but there is nothing in his popular writing that can be construed as a useful framework for
research. Rereading Teilhard today, I blush at the supernaturalist jargon I once took so seriously. In his famous review
of Teilhard's *The Phenomenon of Man*, the distinguished biologist Sir Peter Medawar found nothing to like and much to
detest. The book, he said, "is written in an all but totally
unintelligible style, and this is construed as prima-facie evidence of profundity." Ouch! But, yes, Teilhard's prose does
now seem that of a man who is trying to have his supernaturalist cake and eat his science, too, the same old theology
of sin and salvation tricked up in pseudoscientific jargon.
Even Sir Julian Huxley, who wrote the introduction to the
English edition of *The Phenomenon of Man*, professed himself unable to follow Teilhard "all the way in his gallant
attempt to reconcile the supernatural elements in
Christianity with the facts and implications of evolution."

But let me not be ungenerous—to Teilhard or to my
younger self. Teilhard was there when I needed a guide to
show the way. Behind his breathless Godspeak, one senses
even today a person—like his fellow Jesuit Hopkins—caught
between rebellion and obedience, struggling against the
authority of his Church, yet trying to honor tradition. In this
he is not so far from those of us who seek a reconciliation of
science and spirit. Teilhard was a scientist, yes, and not a bad
one at that, but he was first and foremost a poet and mystic.
His great gift *as a man of faith* was to embrace unhesitatingly
the scientific story of creation, and for this we honor him. He
began with the evolving *fire*—the Heraclitean fire that burns
beyond the dark glass of our ignorance—and drew it down
into the heart of his Darwinian world.

chapter four

On Saying "I Don't Know"

Take the train from London's Victoria Station to the town of Orpington, fourteen miles south of the city. Here you might catch a bus or a taxi for the next leg of your journey, but I chose to set out on foot across the English countryside, down leafy lanes, across grassy meadows. My goal: the picturebook village of Downe, and, nearby, Down House, Charles Darwin's home for forty years. Here he and his wife Emma raised a large, happy family, and here Charles wrote the book that exploded on Victorian culture like a bombshell: *On the Origin of Species by Means of Natural Selection.* The house is today in the care of English Heritage and has been lovingly restored to what it was like when the great man and his family were in residence. His study is as it was when Darwin sat in his chair penning the

155,000 words that would revolutionize our understanding of our place in nature; every flat surface of the study is covered with the tools and collections of a curious mind—fossils, flints, plant specimens, books, microscope. The greenhouse at the back of the house is stuffed with plants, as it was in Darwin's day. At the rear of the property is the "Sand Walk," where Charles would go to stroll and ponder the significance of his exhaustive—and exhausting—observations.

He was not a well man. He suffered constantly and terribly from debilitating symptoms that may or may not have been mostly psychosomatic. He sent his book off into the world, and, as all of England debated its import, he carried on with his latest research, on creeping plants, trying to figure out how they evolved. His biographers Adrian Desmond and James Moore write:

> Tables and sills were an entangled mass of twiners and tendrils; pots perched on every ledge as he timed sweeps and tested the effects of light. Warm summer days were spent in the hop fields watching the plants snake up their poles. He brought hops inside, and sat ill in bed tying weights to their tips in an attempt to slow their ascent. Around the house the vines took on a surreal appearance, covered in paint markers as he timed their twisting movements.

On my visit to Down House I sat for a long time in the sunny back garden and imagined Darwin across the way in the greenhouse, in black hat and cape, crouched over pots of twiners, measuring and recording every twist and turn of the tendrils fingering upwards. Were the stem-twiners and the tendril-wavers related, and if so, how? Were the grasping hooks of the climbers modified leaf stems? How did the twisting and the hooking aid the plants in their struggle for existence? Sixteen miles to the north in London, churches, newspaper offices, scientific societies, classrooms, and drawing rooms were stirred by *Origin of Species* into an uproar of contention and indignation: If all living things were related by common descent from a primeval ancestor, what made humankind unique? If chance and struggle shaped the tree of life, what was the role of Divine Providence? Oblivious to the turmoil, Darwin tended his creepers and twiners.

For most of Darwin's contemporaries, the twining plants were no more of a mystery than any other feature of the natural world. Everything was the work of a supernatural Creator during the six biblical days of creation. Nothing was hidden. A single explanation sufficed: *God did it.*

God did it was not satisfactory for Darwin. He sought a story of the past that invoked no agency *except those that we see at work in the world today,* a single story that embraced the hills, the valleys, the myriad fossil organisms with their similarities and differences, and, of course, his twining plants. As for the agency behind the story, he was content to say, "I don't know."

Those three little words—"I don't know"—may be science's most important contribution to human civilization. Yes, we have learned an astonishing amount about how the world works, but of equal significance is our growing awareness of how much we don't know. Darwin was not adverse to confessing his ignorance, and he did so frequently in his many letters to family and friends. He was especially ready to admit his innocence with regard to the big questions, the questions traditionally addressed by religion: *Why is there something rather than nothing? Why are the laws of nature what they are? Who am I? Where did I come from? What does it all mean?* Darwin was deeply conscious of the mystery of existence, and reluctant to cover his ignorance with myth and fables. He devoted his life unstintingly to peeling back the veil that hides the goddess, but he was not ready to give a name to what remained concealed. In a letter to the American biologist Asa Gray, Darwin wrote:

I am inclined to look at everything as resulting from designed laws, with the details, whether good or bad, left to the working out of what we may call chance. Not that this notion at all satisfies me. I feel most deeply that the whole subject is too profound for the human intellect. A dog might as well speculate on the mind of Newton. Let each man hope and believe what he can.

The physicist Heinz Pagels might have been describing Charles Darwin when he wrote:

The capacity to tolerate complexity and welcome contradiction, not the need for simplicity and certainty, is the attribute of an explorer. Centuries ago, when some people suspended their search for absolute truth and began instead to ask how things worked, modern science was born. Curiously, it was by abandoning the search for absolute truth that science began to make progress, opening the material universe to human exploration.

Although Heraclitus told us thousands of years ago that nature loves to hide, awareness of our ignorance is a very modern thing. Awareness of ignorance is a door to mystery, an invitation to a lifelong affair with the teasing goddess. Darwin counted himself an agnostic, but in his reverence for the creative agency of nature we should count him a devoutly religious man. "There is a grandeur in this view of life," he famously wrote on the last page of *Origin of Species*; the grandeur Darwin spoke of has more of the divine about it than did the anthropomorphic idol who occupied the thoughts of his contemporaries.

The seventeenth-century French philosopher Blaise Pascal is perhaps best known for his *Pensées* (Thoughts), a grab bag of platitudes, nonsense and substance, a disorganized sketch of the book Pascal might have written had he lived long enough (he died at age thirty-nine). Disorganized, yes, but the *Pensées* contains enough nuggets of wisdom to have won it a place among Western classics. One entry I have always liked is this:

> Scientific learning is composed of two opposites which nonetheless meet each other. The first is the natural ignorance that is man's lot at birth. The second is represented by those great minds that have investigated all knowledge accumulated by man only to discover at the end that in fact they know nothing. Thus they return to the same fundamental ignorance they had thought to leave. Yet this ignorance they have now discovered is an intellectual achievement. It is those who have departed from their original condition of ignorance but have been incapable of completing the full cycle of learning who offer us a smattering of scientific knowledge and pass sweeping judgments. These are the mischief makers, the false prophets. (*Pensées* V:327)

Pascal is suggesting that the purpose of science—and indeed of all learning—is to arrive at a state of ignorance, but *an ignorance that is aware of itself.* It took almost three centuries for this remarkable insight to become the common opinion of scientists. The twentieth-century philosopher Karl Popper expressed it this way:

> The more we learn about the world, and the deeper our learning, the more conscious, specific, and articulate will be our knowledge of what we do not know, our knowledge of our ignorance. For this, indeed, is the main source of our ignorance—the fact that our knowledge can be only finite, while our ignorance must necessarily be infinite.

The physician/essayist Lewis Thomas went further: "The greatest of all the accomplishments of twentieth-century science has been the discovery of human ignorance."

It is an odd, unsettling thought that the culmination of the scientific quest—the long, slow gathering of reliable empirical knowledge of the world—should be confirmation of how *little* we understand about the universe we live in. If the writers I have quoted above are correct, the essence of wisdom is the willingness to say "I don't know." Why does Bach's St. Matthew Passion reduce me to awed silence? *I don't know.* Why does the sight of a darting tree swallow make me grin with delight? *I don't know.* Maybe someday we will know the answers to these questions, but for the moment, "I don't know."

On the other hand, consider all the questions for which we now have answers, which were formerly mysterious. Why does the sun sometimes go dark at midday? Why does the comet appear in the sky? Why a plague? Why drought? Why the infestation of locusts? Whence the mountains and the valleys? Why the fossils on the mountaintop? How did the universe begin? As long as our answers to these questions invoked gods or supernatural agents—as they did for thousands of years, and still do for most people—no reliable public knowledge was possible. Only when a few curious people said "I don't know" did science begin. Recognition of our ignorance is a prerequisite of scientific discovery.

In an earlier book (*Honey from Stone*) I used the metaphor of knowledge as an island in a sea of mystery. Since the sea is effectively (perhaps actually) infinite, the growth of the island does not deplete our ignorance. Rather, it increases the shoreline along which we may encounter mystery. Subsequent to using that metaphor, I discovered that it isn't original; in fact, it has an illustrious history. So far, the first use of the metaphor that I have discovered is by the eighteenth-century English scientist Joseph Priestley, the discoverer of oxygen, who wrote:

> The greater is the circle of light, the greater is the boundary of the darkness by which it is confined. But, notwithstanding this, the more light we get, the more thankful we ought to be, for by this means we have the greater range for satisfactory contemplation. In time,

the bounds of light will be still further extended; and from the infinity of the divine nature, and the divine works, we may promise ourselves an endless progress in our investigation of them: a prospect truly sublime and glorious.

As Pascal suggested, in our infancy and youth we are indoctrinated into the traditional beliefs of our tribe—beliefs as various as tribal gods are various. Many of us live all our lives in thrall to the traditions in which we are born. Others question their tribal inheritance and embark upon a lifetime of exploration. The former end up believing they know everything. The latter end as they began, in ignorance—but now a willingly-professed ignorance that is sublime in its tentatively-held and ever-expanding wealth of knowledge.

Who am I? Why am I here? What does it all mean? The Big Questions. There was a time in my life, as an ignorant youngster, when I was happy to be given answers. It is the human condition to want answers. Now, having lived through the Pascalean cycle, I am content to say "I don't know." Like all of us, I began as a newborn babe in ignorance. Like some of us, I end in ignorance, but an ignorance that is (dare I hope?) a kind of wisdom. I no longer require answers to the Big Questions. I want instead answers to the Little Questions. How do the enzymes in every cell of my body build proteins, carbohydrates, and lipids? How do helium nuclei form carbon nuclei in the cores of stars, releasing energy? How does a hummingbird hover? "The Tao that can be told is not the eternal Tao," wrote Lao Tzu, two-and-a-half thousand years ago. The name that can be named is not the eternal name. Let me celebrate here and now what can be told and named, and let the eternal Tao remain mysterious.

In a 1931 letter to his sister, the celebrated paleontologist George Gaylord Simpson was pondering the ultimate scientific question, how did the universe begin?

Call that great Unknowable by any name you wish, call it X, or Yahweh, or God, or say that God created it. Applying the letters "g", "o", and "d" to it or what created it is no explanation and no consolation. It is a common failing, even more among scientists than among laymen, to think that naming a thing explains it, or that we know a thing because we can put a name to it. But to say that God created the universe means nothing whatever.

Faced with the mystery of the big bang—which remains today as inexplicable as it was in Simpson's time—the empirical naturalist will say "I don't know." Perhaps an explanation will come along, perhaps not, but to say, "God did it," adds nothing to our understanding. "If a sign is useless, it is meaningless," said Wittgenstein. God? X? It is all the same. Take your pick, but do not suppose that you have anything to worship but a hollow idol. The eternal Tao remains mysterious. Nature loves to hide.

Names, of course, are necessary, even for mysteries that are deep beyond our knowing. There can be no theory of the electron, for example, until we have a word for the electron. But naming is not understanding. Before we say we understand a thing, we must weave it into a web of concepts that constitutes a theory. Only when the concept "electron" is enmeshed in a matrix of other ideas—atoms, fields, valency, molecular bonds, etc.—by *taut, quantitative, empirical connections*, do we have confidence that we know what an electron is. Only when the concept "electron" permits the doing of an experiment—a needle twitches as predicted on a meter, perhaps—do we feel confident that electrons are "real."

Is there a circularity in scientific explanation? Yes. Every explanatory system refers back upon itself. It is the *timbre* of the web and the way the web makes empirical verification possible that give us confidence that we are doing something right. To say that "God" caused the big bang predicts *absolutely nothing* about what we should see when we turn our telescopes to the most distant universe. No needle twitches. The threads that connect the concept "God" to the earliest universe are infinitely slack. Not so the physical theory of the big bang, which predicted precisely the resulting electromagnetic radiation that should fill the universe—the so-called cosmic microwave background radiation—*before* the radiation was observed. The agreement between the predicted and observed energy spectrums is breathtaking.

The biologist Richard Dawkins once asked a distinguished astronomer to explain the big bang theory. "He did so to the best of his (and my) ability," says Dawkins, "and I then asked what it was about the fundamental laws of physics that made the spontaneous origin of space and time possible. 'Ah,' smiled the astronomer, 'now we move beyond the realm of science. This is where I have to hand you over to our good friend, the chaplain.'" But why the chaplain? asks Dawkins. Why not the gardener or the chef? And with his usual incisive wit Dawkins cuts to the chase. The gardener, chef, astronomer, and chaplain are equally ignorant of how the universe began. The chaplain says "God"; the astronomer says "I don't know." The two responses have exactly the same explanatory content.

Zero.

Thomas Henry Huxley, Darwin's nineteenth-century champion, once described how he came to originate the term *agnosticism*:

> When I reached intellectual maturity, and began to ask myself whether I was an atheist, a theist, or a pantheist; a materialist or an idealist; a Christian or a freethinker, I found that the more I learned and reflected, the less ready was the answer; until at last I came to the conclusion that I had neither art nor part with any of these denominations, except the last. The one thing in which most of these good people were agreed was the one thing in which I differed from them. They were quite

sure that they had attained a certain "gnosis" [knowledge of hidden mysteries]—had more or less successfully solved the problem of existence; while I was quite sure I had not, and had a pretty strong conviction that the problem was insoluble. . . . So I took thought, and invented what I conceived to be the appropriate title of "agnostic". It came into my head as suggestively antithetic to the "gnostic" of Church history, who professed to know so much about the very things of which I was ignorant.

Huxley had come full circle to the place described by Pascal: an awareness of his own ignorance. Agnosticism, he insisted, is not a creed, but a method. "Positively the principle may be expressed: In matters of the intellect, follow your reason as far as it will take you, without regard to any other consideration. And negatively: In matters of the intellect, do not pretend that conclusions are certain which are not demonstrated or demonstrable." This might seem a thin foundation upon which to stand a life, and indeed it takes a certain courage to make one's way in the world without the buttress of true belief. Huxley himself was sorely pressed by adversities, including the deaths of beloved children, but he found the courage to endure and to prevail. He said that if a man stays true to the agnostic principle, with humility, as best he could, "he shall not be ashamed to look the universe in the face, whatever the future may have in store for him."

Charles Darwin, too, after a lifetime of learning arrived at an agnostic ignorance. And he too faced afflictions without the support of belief in a loving God or an afterlife, most particularly the death of his darling daughter Annie at age ten, apparently of tuberculosis. With Annie's death, the great biologist at last put the notion of a personal divinity behind him. He too had completed the circle of Pascal. He was one of those "great minds that have investigated all knowledge accumulated by man only to discover at the end that in fact they know nothing." Darwin unveiled as much of nature's hidden mystery as any person before or after. And having seen as deeply as anyone into the secrets that nature is wont to hide, he knew that ultimate knowledge receded from his grasp. There was no gnosis, no revelation, no church or holy book, that could take him to a place where Annie's death might be ameliorated. But even in his grievous bereavement he continued to see "the face of nature bright with gladness."

The Sea
Into Which
All Rivers Flow

Religion, magic, science: All assume a reality behind the commonplace that gives meaning and structure to the world, and which might somehow be made to work for our benefit. Thus we have offered prayers, incense, and sacrifice to the gods, cast magical spells and incantations, or built, for example, colossally expensive particle accelerators to probe the inner secrets of atoms and the first moments of the ultra-hot big bang.

To what effect? As for prayer, the gods have been dramatically nonforthcoming, given the vast amount of attention and resources we have proffered on their behalf; they smite us with the same afflictions whether we attend their altars or not—and not a shred of non-anecdotal evidence suggests otherwise. Magic was a preferred way of reaching

37

behind nature's veil for countless generations, but it is now universally recognized as a sham, confined with a wink and a nod to the likes of David Copperfield. Meanwhile, the experimental methods of science have gone from success to success. We send space probes to distant planets and they land on a dime. We reproduce the first moments of the big bang with machines so big they dwarf the largest of the medieval cathedrals.

There was a time when the world was universally thought to be full of active spirits, heavenly influences, and intrusions of divine will. All of that sounds superstitious to modern ears, but when you think about it, is it any less astonishing that we believe (know!) that the very space in which we live our lives is resonant with thousands of immaterial vibrations bearing in their various frequencies music, news, telephone conversations, Internet access. Radio waves are no less amazing, on the face of it, than body auras or poltergeists, but who will deny that with the experimental discovery and manipulation of electromagnetic radiation, science has tapped into *and controlled* something fundamental and real. All the prayers and magic in the world would not connect my laptop wirelessly to the Internet.

But the experimental method has not gone unchallenged, and we should pay particular attention to the critique of science that has gone by the name "romantic reaction"—as represented, for example, by the poet Goethe—lest the hubris that comes with experimental success blinds us to the sensate pleasures of the commonplace, on the one hand, and mystery, on the other.

Johann Wolfgang Goethe was a polymath who counted himself a scientist as well as a poet. He developed a theory of colors and wrote on the geography of plants. Few aspects of the world escaped his insatiable curiosity. But he was not part of mainstream nineteenth-century science. He never achieved the enduring influence of Michael Faraday or Charles Darwin. His success as a scientist was forestalled by his explicit *rejection* of the Heraclitean maxim: Nature loves to hide.

The goddess has no veils, said Goethe. Nothing is hidden. There is a mystery, yes, but it reveals itself in "broad daylight" to anyone with sufficiently acute intuition. He wrote: "Nature has no mystery that she does not place fully naked before the eyes of the attentive observer." One need not build multibillion-dollar particle accelerators or space telescopes to discover nature's secrets. Just open your eyes. What you see is what you get. Goethe famously took Newton to task for his experiments with light, notably for passing white light through a prism and separating it into its component colors. Whatever Newton found thereby, Goethe believed, was not nature as we should seek to know it, but rather a broken, shattered thing. In this he agreed with Wordsworth's famous line, "We murder to dissect."

History has passed judgment on Goethe's science, which led nowhere. The empirical methods of Newton, Faraday, and Darwin gave us the modern world. Nature *does* hide, and some element of violence may be necessary to strip away her veils. Francis Bacon, the great philosopher of experimental science, said that nature must be "put to the torture" to yield her secrets. It is a grim metaphor, very seventeenth-century, and he surely would use a less malevolent image today. But he is correct that nature must be seduced to yield her secrets. The non-experimental observer could attend to the world forever and *never* discover the electromagnetic spectrum, the quantum periodicities of the elements, or the double-spiral of the DNA. Without centuries of dissection of deceased organisms and experiments on living organisms, our health would still be in the hands of faith healers and shamans.

Still, give Goethe this: The experimental method should not distract us from the world of the commonplace in which we live our affective lives. Rather, it should add more layers of affective understanding. Who can look, for example, at the magnificent cosmic images provided by the Hubble Space Telescope and not feel shaken to the core of their affective being. We properly admire Goethe and Wordsworth for the intensity of their engagement with the natural world, but do we really want to live without knowledge of the galaxies and the DNA?

It is one thing to discern—with the Romantics—mystery in a starry night or a child's smile. We also encounter mystery in the lovely harmonics of the periodic table of the elements and the genomic code of the fruit fly. We peel back Nature's veil and find—yes—more of the same natural world that excited Goethe's unaided perceptions, but more too, more of an apparently *inexhaustible* mystery, as layered as an infinite onion, that deserves at every level of knowledge our attention, reverence, thanksgiving, and praise.

Science has proved amazingly adept at revealing nature's secrets. But at what risk? The romantic poets and some contemporary environmentalists warn us to let well enough alone. "Is it wise to raise the veil / Where terror, threatening, dwells?" asks Schiller in a poem. The theme goes back to the Garden of Eden: Knowledge can be catastrophic. Pandora's box is best left unopened. The dream of reason brings forth monsters.

There can be no doubt that knowledge confers power, and power imposes responsibilities. Einstein's beautiful work on relativity revealed almost preternaturally the secret of starlight in that extraordinary equation $E = mc^2$, but it also made possible the nightmare of nuclear weapons. Should we therefore back away from knowledge? The only first-rank scientist I know of who has urged restraint in lifting Nature's veil was the grand old man of DNA research Erwin Chargaff, who shortly before his death in 2002 at age ninety-seven warned his colleagues to forego human embryo experimentation. In words shuddering with indignation he chastened fellow scientists who "stick their clumsy fingers into the incredibly fine web of human fate." "Scientific curiosity is not an unbounded good," he thundered. "Restraint in asking necessary questions is one of the sacrifices that even the scientist ought to be willing to make to human dignity."

Curiosity, or restraint? Learn the secrets of the gods and share their power, or be content as humble acolytes of the secret force that rules the universe? That the myths of Promethean hubris are so ancient and so enduring speaks of their profundity. As I write, I am sitting in a shack on a tiny cay in the central Bahamas. The shack has no electricity, no telephone, no plumbing. Outside the window are the turquoise sea, blue sky, gentle breezes. The only sound is the lap of the sea against the rocky shore. Bliss! A feast for the senses. But bliss for only a few hours. Then my laptop battery will run out of power. Twice already this morning I wish I could have logged onto the Internet to check Erwin Chargaff's dates and the exact wording of a Wordsworth aphorism. A few days here without plumbing and my idyll would be overwhelmed by unpleasant odors. For all of the romance of this Edenic place, I am quick to retreat to the house with the scientific and technological amenities. There is no turning back or stopping the empirical method— Romantic protests notwithstanding.

Still, each of us individually will make a choice—to lift the goddess's veil or leave her cloaked. Knowledge with its attendant risks or stasis? If I had to make an *exclusive* choice, would I choose the modern home with clean running water, flush toilet, and wireless Internet connection, or the sweet shack at the edge of a turquoise sea? An idealized future or an idealized past? In his essay "The Conservative," Emerson wrote: "Conservatism makes no poetry, breathes no prayer, has no invention; it is all memory. Reform has no gratitude, no prudence, no husbandry." If any institution—state or church—is to prosper, it must find a way to balance conservatism and reform, past and future, wisdom and wit. "Each is a good half, but an impossible whole," says Emerson. And what is true of institutions, is true in our individual lives. A balance of innovation and conservation is at the heart of organic evolution. The genes conserve; mutation and selection drive life to ever greater diversity and complexity. We can do no better than adopt the creative dynamic of evolution as our own sustaining myth.

If you wanted to divide humankind into two categories, none might be more relevant to the present state of the world than: 1) those who look to the authority of the past, and 2) those who put their hope in the future. In the first category are persons who give their conceptual allegiance to ancestors, holy books, tradition, venerable prophets, elders, shamans, gurus. In the second category are the children of the Scientific Revolution, the spiritual descendants of Francis Bacon and Galileo.

The idea of progress was pretty much an invention of seventeenth-century Europe. Not that the intellectual revolution of that time and place was without precedents—the empirical scholars of Alexandria in the classical world, especially, anticipated the Scientific Revolution. But it was the forward-looking contemporaries of Bacon and Galileo who first systematically doubted the authority of the ancients and contrived an enduring alternative avenue to truth. The sway of ancient authority prior to the Scientific Revolution is demonstrated, for example, by a statute of the medieval Oxford University, which decreed that bachelors and masters who did not follow Aristotle faithfully were liable to a fine of five shillings for every point of divergence. Galileo, of course, ran afoul of the same slavish allegiance to the past in the form of Church doctrine. By contrast, the new scientific savants of the seventeenth century emphasized the inadequacy of ancient learning and urged its advancement. Truth was to be henceforth measured not by conformity with the past, but by an open-ended inquiry of nature. The veils would come off, one by one. In his seminal study of the Scientific Revolution, Richard Foster Jones defined the new movement this way: "First was the spirit of adventure, of finding out what lies beyond the closed boundaries of knowledge, of widening the limits of acquired truth, together with the faith that such expansion was possible. Another attitude stressed the need of an unbiased and critical mind and freedom of thought and expression." These values became the basis for the Enlightenment's commitment to democracy, secularism, individual rights, universal public education, and free speech. They are the foundations of modern medicine, open markets, and the exponential (and sometimes dangerous) growth of technology. The clash of civilizations in the world today is not between socialism and capitalism, or Islam and the West— to give but two widely touted examples—but between the spirit of the Scientific Revolution (which until recently has been identified mostly with the West) and those persons north, east, south, and west who define themselves by the authority of holy books, tradition, or prophets.

What's at stake? Who among us isn't depressed by the sectarian madness that seems to engulf the world, the fury of antagonisms between peoples of different religions and cultures. There is nothing new in any of this; thus it has always been. Is there any chance that we might rid ourselves of this irrational fear of the other? Only if we can find a way to generate reliable *consensus* knowledge of the world. Such a methodology exists, of course, and it is called science. It is the basis for modern technological civilization, but it has so far had only minimal influence of the way most people conduct their lives. In his introduction to Michael Shermer's book *Why People Believe Weird Things*, the late great biologist Stephen Jay Gould wrote:

Only two possible escapes can save us from the organized mayhem of our dark potentialities—the side that has given us crusades, witch hunts, enslavements, and holocausts. Moral decency provides one necessary ingredient, but not nearly enough. The second foundation must come from the rational side of our mentality. For, unless we rigorously use human reason to discover and acknowledge nature's factuality . . . we will lose out to the frightening forces of irrationality, romanticism, uncompromising "true" belief, and the apparent resulting inevitability of mob action.

One of the most compelling spokespersons for consensus knowledge is the Indian philosopher Meera Nanda. Her book *Prophets Facing Backwards: Postmodern Critiques of Science and Hindu Nationalism in India* is richly rewarding, and of exceptional relevance to our time. Nanda champions the *universality* of science as a remedy for cultural fragmentation, and especially as a counterpoint to local truth systems that presume access to the mind of God.

She disputes, for example, the Indian nationalist claim to modernity based on the Vedic "science" of Hindu holy books. Traditional Hindu practices such as astrology, *vastu shastra* (buildings constructed in alignment with a cosmic "life-force"), *ayurveda* (traditional Hindu medicine), transcendental meditation, faith healing, and telepathy merely pretend to the mantle of science says Nanda. In fact, they have nothing in common with science as practiced—first in the West, then globally—since the Scientific Revolution and Enlightenment. Vedic science, she asserts, is a phony face on age-old superstitions.

If all of this sounds familiar, well, that's Nanda's broader point. Think Western postmodernism, with its emphasis on the relativism of truth systems (it matters not a whit whether one believes in the big bang or Coyote tossing stars into the sky, say the relativists). Think intelligent design, astrology, homeopathy, and other pseudoscientific enthusiasms so widely embraced in the West, even among the highly educated classes. Think about the evangelical preachers who promise an imminent Rapture into Eternal Bliss if only one will be born again.

When intellectuals east or west exalt local truth systems over the universality of science, there is nothing left to prevent society's slide into tribalism, religious sectarianism, and nationalist passion, says Nanda. A glance around the world today, with its plethora of religious and ethnic hatreds, suggests that an empirical, secular way of knowing that makes no reference to the gods or to accidents of birth is a gift beyond price. It is a gift that is everywhere under assault.

What looks like tolerant, nonjudgmental "permission to be different" on behalf of Western postmodern intellectuals, is in fact an act of condescension toward non-Western cultures, says Nanda: "It denies them the capacity and the need for a reasoned modification of inherited cosmologies in the light of better evidence made available by the methods of modern science." The postmodern injunction to prefer cultural authenticity over scientific objectivity plays into the hands of religious and cultural nationalists who sow the seeds of violent reaction. Christian "dominionism" in the United States, Hindu nationalism in India, and Islamic jihadism march hand in hand to the same backward-facing piper.

Nanda's critique is particularly valuable for us in the West precisely because her arguments are directed first of all against a "foreign" culture—the dreaded "other." As Nanda analyzes the shortcomings of Hindu nationalism, we say, "Yeah, right on, Nanda, all that superstition and strange theology is bunk." Then we stop and think for a moment and recognize ourselves. It is also important, I think, to hear an Indian philosopher speak so forcefully in favor of Enlightenment values. Nanda evokes an image of the

historian of Chinese science, Joseph Needham: Modern natural science is the sea into which all the rivers of local sciences flow. She writes: "While all medieval, pre-Galilean
sciences, whether from Europe, Asia, or Africa, explained
nature through anthropomorphic metaphors peculiar to
their time and place, modern science alone managed to
break free from time and place." Modern science has
become the *lingua franca* for natural philosophers and scientists around the world, and, for Nanda, that's all for the better. Any way of knowing that secularizes and disenchants
nature works on behalf of oppressed peoples everywhere,
she argues, by breaking the hold of those whose claim to
dominance or special privilege presumes divine favor.

In all of this, Nanda is almost certainly correct. But in a
science-based society, we must ask: What becomes of morality, which has traditionally been based on the precepts of
holy books? What becomes of a sense of the sacred, which
has traditionally been associated with the supernatural?
Nanda addresses these questions too.

Human values and purposes need not, any longer, be
dictated by church, state, custom, or tradition, she says.
Rather, as John Dewey suggested, the success of modern
science shows that human beings are capable of creating
their own regulative standards by subjecting social experience to a collective, democratically conducted inquiry. One
might reasonably argue, following Nanda, that this accounts
for the success of the American national experiment, which
is based on the Enlightenment ideal of equal rights and justice for all.

In Buddhist naturalistic philosophy Nanda finds a world
view with a sense of the sacred that does not offend reason,
and which provides a foundation for a sustainable relationship between humans and the planet that is our home.
There is an equivalent tradition in the West, although it is
very much a minority view, and in the final chapters of this

book I will delineate this alternative paradigm. I will try to show that we can rid ourselves of ancient superstitions and tribal gods and still cultivate a sense of the sacred. A secular, science-based idea of what it means to be human "puts a high premium on reducing all avoidable suffering and on affirming the ordinary life of here-and-now," writes Nanda. When we are content to admit that we do not know what lies behind the goddess's veil, every jot and tittle of creation becomes an object of our reverence and respect.

Wielding Ockham's Razor

At dinner the other evening we were discussing why scientists are so much less likely than the general population to believe in God. Apparently, according to polls, about nine out of ten Americans are believers. Among the members of the National Academy of Scientists, that ratio is reversed.

My daughter's husband posited, only half in jest, "Overweening hubris?"

We laughed. Well, yes, there could be some of that.

My daughter then wondered, "What does *ween* mean?"

And although we had heard or used the expression "overweening hubris" all of our lives, we didn't know.

So to the dictionary. Ween: *v. tr. archaic,* be of the opinion, to suppose.

Overweening then means to be arrogantly of the opinion, overconfident in one's suppositions. Overweening hubris is redundant, but a grand phrase nevertheless.

Is it possible to be underweening? Too unassuming in one's opinions?

We decided that *ween* may be a good word to bring back into the language, to represent the intellectual posture that goes with good science: confidence that our theories represent reality ever more closely, but knowing that every scientific theory is tentative and subject to change. "I ween that the big bang happened." "I ween that life on Earth arose from inanimate matter." Not overweening. Not underweening. Cautious confidence that what we ween is true.

Most people think first of all about *what* they know, not *how* and *why* they know it. It is a characteristic of most traditionally religious people, for example, that apologetics (justifying what we know) comes before epistemology (thinking about *how* and *why* we know).

In science, epistemology takes precedence.

First we ask, "What are reliable grounds for belief? What is the role of logic? Empiricism? Skepticism? Peer review? How do we guard against cultural or innate prejudices? Which version of the truth can amass the most universal consensus among people of diverse geographical and cultural backgrounds?" People who hold religious beliefs without first having studied epistemology seldom consider, for example, that the factor that correlates most closely with their beliefs is the circumstance of their birth. The vast majority of Christians were born Christians; the vast majority of Muslims were born Muslims; and so on. By contrast, epistemology asks, "Are the circumstances of one's birth a reliable guide to truth?" The motto of the first modern scientific organization, the Royal Society of seventeenth-century London was: "Don't take anyone's word"; authority and tradition were deemed unreliable guarantors of truth. Why? Because authority and tradition are as various as cultures are various. Surely truth, if we can find it, will be independent of cultural context. Or so believed the founders of the scientific way of knowing, and the stunning successes of their methodology would appear to confirm their intuition. Can you imagine any traditional knowledge system that would have led to the discovery of the galaxies or DNA?

Only when we have first established a satisfying epistemology should we commit ourselves to belief—and then only tentatively. That is the message of science.

When belief comes first, one can always amass a body of anecdotal lore to justify what one believes. When I was an undergraduate at the University of Notre Dame in the 1950s, a required course in apologetics was part of the curriculum. Our text was Frank Sheed's *Theology and Sanity*, the theme of which was: If you don't recognize the truths of Catholic theology, you are insane. Which meant, of course, that most of the world's population was insane, and only we Roman Catholics were illuminated. Our teachers did not mention that most of us in that apologetics course were there because we had been born into Roman Catholic families. (I almost said "born Roman Catholics," but of course no child is born a believer of any religion; we are all indoctrinated into a faith.) Fortunately, along with apologetics, Notre Dame provided me with an excellent course in epistemology and—bless 'em—a sound scientific education.

What is science? I would emphasize consensus: Science is the attempt by skeptical and curious men and women—let's call them scientists—to gain *consensus* knowledge of the world, by trying as best they can to minimize cultural bias (tradition, religion, politics, ethnicity, gender, etc.) and letting nature have its say. It is precisely because scientific knowledge is first of all *consensus* knowledge that nonscientists can embrace it with confidence. And, of course, if we are honest, we recognize that modern medicine, sanitation, and technology stand as monuments to the effectiveness of the scientific way of knowing.

To achieve consensus, scientists have devised a number of tools to ply their trade: quantitative observation, mathematical language, peer review, institutionalized doubt, and, of course, the willingness to say "I don't know." There is something else, something fundamental to the scientific way of knowing, something which in the last analysis is the philosophical foundation upon which the whole enterprise stands: the principle of parsimony. Or, as it is more generally known, Ockham's razor.

William of Ockham was a fourteenth-century English Franciscan friar and philosopher, from the tiny village of Ockham in Surrey (the village still lies just beyond the sprawl of metropolitan London). He was educated at London and Oxford, and preached and taught across Europe. He is known today almost exclusively because his name is attached to the principle of philosophical parsimony: Never suppose a complex explanation when a simpler explanation will suffice. Ockham was not the first to enunciate this principle, but he wielded the razor to great advantage, shaving away superfluous accretions from the philosophy and theology of his time—an exercise that ultimately earned him excommunication from the Church he served.

Ockham's razor is a bedrock principle of modern science. Newton put it this way: "We are to admit no more causes of natural things than such as are both true and sufficient to explain their appearance." And Einstein: "The grand aim of science . . . is to cover the greatest possible number of empirical facts by logical deductions from the smallest possible number of hypotheses of axioms." Simplicity. Parsimony. The razor is not something that can be *proved* by reason or empirical evidence, despite the best efforts of Ockham and other medieval philosophers. After all, from the point of view of medieval philosophy, God's omnipotence means he could have created the world by few principles or many. If there is a "proof" of the razor, it is in the pudding. By ruthlessly paring away superfluous entities in our understanding of the world—including, most dramatically, gods, miracles, and the supernatural—science has given us the modern world.

Someone once quoted Shakespeare to the philosopher W. V. O. Quine: "There are more things in heaven and earth than are dreamt of in your philosophy." The remark was meant as a put-down, a sort of "Yeah, Mr. Quine, so what do you know?" To which Quine is said to have responded: "Possibly, but my concern is that there not be more things in my philosophy than are in heaven and earth." Quine was an Ockhamist. On the other hand, in a certain episode of *The X-Files*, Fox Mulder dismisses Ockham's razor by renaming it Ockham's Principle of Unimaginative Thinking. Let a thousand paranormal and pseudoscientific flowers bloom, Mulder seems to be saying. Gods, angels, spirits, extraterrestrials, alien abductions, UFOs, ESP, channelers, mind over matter, immaterial souls, life after death, miracles, the Rapture: Anything goes. Mulder is an anti-Ockhamist.

The Ockhamist does not look to miracles or the paranormal when a natural explanation will suffice. And when no natural explanation presents itself (as, for example, "What is the origin of the big bang?"), the Ockhamist will say, simply, "I don't know." To admit our ignorance in the face of nature's prodigality is a very different thing than filling our ignorance with agencies of our own invention. Or so we were taught by the poor, brown-robed, sandal-clad friar from Ockham who stands—could he have imagined such a thing?—as our champion of intellectual humility.

Ockham's razor, wisely applied, has proved a royal road to practical, reliable, consensus knowledge of the world. Since the time of Galileo, and especially since the Enlightenment, it has been the basis for our health, wealth, and general happiness. And—Fox Mulder notwithstanding—the razor is our most powerful tool in the battle against the darker demons of sectarian strife, religious triumphalism, and pseudoscientific superstition.

Why is the scientific community so unwelcoming to New Age gurus and peddlers of the paranormal such as Rupert Sheldrake, Russell Targ, Deepak Chopra, and Harold Puthoff? The answer, simply: Ockham's razor. Only when the preachers and the gurus can show that an effect is real and reproducible (as opposed to anecdotal), and that the existing body of scientific lore is not sufficient to explain it, will nature's laws be amended to accommodate their pet enthusiasms.

Let me take just one example of a popular author who could do with a good shave of the razor. Larry Dossey is among the best-selling alternative medicine practitioners. In his book *Healing Words* he suggests an answer to the question I posed in the previous paragraph. The answer, he writes, "has less to do with the quality of the [alternative medicine] data than with the psychology of scientists themselves." That is to say, scientists are skeptical of the claims of alternative medicine because of limitations of their attitude or methodology—Mulder's Principle of Unimaginative Thinking, so to speak. Dossey then offers a dozen reasons why scientists reject the "evidence" for the healing power of prayer:

1. Western materialistic beliefs exclude the possibility of prayer-based healing.
2. It is human nature to resist change.
3. Cognitive dissonance (the discomfort people feel when there is a conflict between their perceptions and their belief system).
4. Spiritual healing is often equated with "mysticism."

5. Prayer-type healing may occur outside of conscious control.
6. The "power of others" may be feared (to influence our lives negatively).
7. One's own healing powers may be feared.
8. Healing power is believed to be possessed only by people who are strange or different.
9. The lack of replicability of healing phenomena.
10. Healing has laws that appear to differ from those of other sciences.
11. Healing is often allied with specific religions that emphasize faith and belief.
12. Careers and financial investments are at stake.

Well, this represents a formidable indictment of scientific skepticism. Let me comment on each of these purported reasons why most scientists are suspicious of psychic and divine healing. What I have to say generally applies to other New Age pseudosciences and to the claims of supernaturalist religion:

1. *Western materialistic beliefs exclude the possibility of prayer-based healing.* Certainly, states of mind affect the body—there is ample evidence of *that*—but there is at present no conceptual framework *within science* that makes *remote* prayer-based healing likely. If thoughts can influence living organisms *at a distance*, then we have missed something very fundamental about the way the world works. To accommodate such effects, a major scientific revolution would be necessary. Revolutions in science do occur, but only when the data suggesting change is overwhelming. As the astronomer Carl Sagan said: "Extraordinary claims require extraordinary evidence." So far, claims for psychic or divine healing are not convincing, relying almost

entirely on anecdote or statistically and procedurally suspect experiments that are unreproducible by skeptics. To compromise the fabulously successful intellectual underpinnings of science on the basis of statistically marginal and irreproducible experiments would be folly.

2. *It is human nature to resist change.* True. And this is certainly a danger in science, as in every human enterprise. Any reliable way of knowing *must* be conservative to some extent; if every idea is awarded equal currency in the marketplace of ideas, then no progress towards truth is possible. A good rule of thumb is this: Any reliable truth system must be radically open to marginal change, and marginally open to radical change. Admitting psychic or divine healing into the belief system of contemporary science would be radical change, to be undertaken only when the weight of evidence in overwhelming.

3. *Cognitive dissonance (the discomfort people feel when there is a conflict between their perceptions and their belief system).* Yes, of course, cognitive dissonance applies as much to individual scientists as to anyone else. This is why the scientific way of knowing is organized as a collective enterprise, and why all references to religion, politics, gender, etc., are excluded from scientific communication. The goal of science is that every idea will have its feet held firmly to the fire of collective empirical scrutiny.

4. *Spiritual healing is often equated with "mysticism."* Spiritual healing, quantum healing, and so on, do indeed smack of the processions, prayers, self-flagellations, holy water, and blessings that characterized pre-scientific medicine (more on this later). Scientists are rightfully cautious about

avoiding a slippery slope that would lead back into "mysticism."

5. *Prayer-type healing may occur outside of conscious control.* Dossey's implication is that scientists are control freaks, resisting anything that involves the workings of the unconscious. He is right, in this sense: The controlled experiment, consciously designed and executed, is the gold standard of science. Unless, and until, psychic or divine healing manifests itself reliably in controlled experiments performed (or evaluated favorably) by skeptics, it is unlikely to find a place in the scientific world view.

6. *The "power of others" may be feared (to influence our lives negatively).* This may operate with individual scientists, but it is hard to see how it could significantly affect the collective enterprise.

7. *One's own healing powers may be feared.* Ditto.

8. *Healing power is believed to be possessed only by people who are strange or different.* Rational people are rightly skeptical of ideas that are preferentially embraced by supermarket tabloid newspapers. Dossey says: "People who are uncomfortable with healing may attribute these powers to mediums, guides, channelers, kooks, weirdos, or religious nuts." Yes, and perhaps scientists are rightly skeptical of ideas that kooks, weirdos, and religious nuts preferentially embrace.

9. *Lack of replicability of healing phenomena.* Dossey admits: "It is true that healers have not been able to reproduce results with reliability and consistency." And here is the crux of the matter. "Science accepts many phenomena that are inherently unpredictable, from electrons to earthquakes," says Dossey. And it is true that electrons obey

quantum laws that are not deterministic in the classical sense, but we can perform experiments with electrons that exhibit exceptional reliability and consistency. Our entire electronic lifestyle is based on the reliability and consistency of electronics. Earthquakes cannot be individually predicted reliably, but the laws of rock fracture and slip are understood with great reliability, and even a cursory glance at a global earthquake occurrence map shows the power of plate tectonics to account collectively for quakes.

10. *Healing has laws that appear to differ from those of other sciences.* Psychic and divine healing have no laws. If and when such laws can be reliably demonstrated, you can be sure that science will be amended to incorporate these phenomena.

11. *Healing is often allied with specific religions that emphasize faith and belief.* True. Science has succeeded (as have the Western democracies) by defining and defending itself as a secular enterprise.

12. *Careers and financial investments are at stake.* Of course this applies to individual scientists, to scientific labs, and perhaps even to entire fields of research. But bear in mind that it also applies to the Larry Dosseys, Deepak Chopras, and other purveyors of books and lectures advocating alternative healing therapies. No one is immune to the foibles of human nature, which—again—is the very reason science insists upon reproducible experimental evidence.

Now, having established the basis for scientific skepticism, shouldn't we examine the evidence Dossey presents for psychic healing? Before his death, professor emeritus of psychology at the University of Kentucky Robert Baker examined the 131 laboratory experiments compiled by Daniel Benor and offered by Dossey in support of psychic influences on living organisms (yeast cells, algae, insect larva, plants, and animals). The cited experiments are in almost every case only marginally statistically significant and unreproducible by skeptics. Baker writes: "When we consider the quality and credibility of these studies we find that ten of these are unpublished doctoral dissertations, two are unpublished master's theses, and all of the rest were published in parapsychological journals." So, to start with, even before we start invoking explanations that stand in violation of the razor, we find that there is not much to explain.

But, if the experiments cited by Dossey are non-reproducible, why did the experimenters see results in the first place?

Four centuries ago, Francis Bacon said that what a person would like to be true, he preferentially believes. Even the most fair-minded observer can be led into error by unconscious or unexamined prejudices, which is why scientists place so much emphasis on controlled experiments, reproducibility, the statistical analysis of data, peer review, mathematics, diagrams, photographs, specialized languages, and the strict exclusion of personal, religious, and political affiliations from scientific communication. The point of these strategies is to minimize the effect of "seeing what we want to see."

But no knowledge system, not even science, can be entirely free of personal and cultural predispositions. The history of science is full of wrong turns taken on the basis of personal or cultural prejudices. A subtle example of how easy it is to misjudge evidence is the work of the astronomer Adriaan van Maanen on the rotation of galaxies. It's worth a look.

In the second decade of the last century, one of the biggest unanswered questions in astronomy was the distance to the so-called "spiral nebula," pinwheel-shaped whirls of stars and gas that could be observed with telescopes. You've seen pictures of "spiral nebula"; we now call them spiral galaxies. The big question was: Are the spiral nebulas situated among the stars of the Milky Way Galaxy, which contains the Sun, and therefore relatively nearby and small, or are they far beyond the Milky Way and perhaps as large as the Milky Way Galaxy itself? One way to answer this question was to see if rotational motion could be detected in the spirals. If the spirals are small and nearby, they might appear to rotate more quickly than if they are larger and far away. (It's like comparing the rotation of the disk in my computer's hard drive to the rotation of the Earth. If the Earth rotated at the RPMs of my hard drive, it would fly asunder.)

Van Maanen looked for rotation by comparing photographs of face-on spirals taken some years apart. It was a simple and apparently foolproof task he undertook: compare the positions of stars in two photographs of the same spiral nebula. In spiral after spiral he found consistent evidence of rotation—as if the spiral nebulas were unwinding! The star displacements he observed were tiny but apparently real, and since van Maanen was one of the most respected astronomers in the world for this sort of work, his results were widely accepted. His measurements suggested that the spiral nebula were relatively small and close—and inside the Milky Way, which therefore retained its status as a unique universe of stars.

It took more than a decade for astronomers to realize that van Maanen's consistent and convincing measurements were in error. Others who attempted to reproduce his work were not able to do so. And in the meantime other *independent* ways of estimating the distances to the spiral nebulas indicated that the spirals were *outside* of the Milky Way, and therefore large enough to be other Milky Ways. We now know that the spirals are so far away that it would have been impossible for any investigator to measure the rotation during the time intervals used by van Maanen. Galaxies, we now know, require hundreds of millions of years to complete a full turning.

So what was the source of van Maanen's error? Historians Richard Berendzen, Richard Hart, and Daniel Seeley have examined van Maanen's work (which like the work of any good scientist was recorded in detail and archived for future examination) and ruled out systematic instrumental and computational errors. Their conclusion: It seems that van Maanen had a slight personal bias toward believing that the spirals were unwinding, and his results reflected this bias. In other words, while this gifted scientist strove for complete objectivity, his measurements were nonetheless affected by his expectations.

The machinery of scientific knowing is designed to prevent or detect exactly this kind of error, and eventually did so in the case of van Maanen's galaxies. The final arbiter of scientific truth is repeatable, reproducible experiment. Nature, not our hopes or desires, must have the last word. And this is what is wrong with the evidence proffered by Dossey and others for "psychic healing" or, for that matter, for the efficacy of petitionary prayer.

One should always be skeptical about experimental results that lie close to the margin of instrumental, statistical, or personal errors. All of the so-called evidence for the efficacy of prayerful or psychic healing falls into this category, and that is why scientists are skeptical. History has taught us how easy it is to see what we want to see.

Albert Einstein said, "Theories should be as simple as possible, but no simpler."

At first glance, this may sound like a Zen koan or a paradox. In fact, it is a profound statement of Ockham's razor.

But first, a bit of background.

From the dawn of time, people have resisted saying: "I don't know." They looked instead for explanations in tribal tradition, sacred books, or the wisdom of shamans, priests, preachers, and prophets. The most common cover for ignorance is to invoke divinity. A storm that devastates a village is "an act of God." A child is taken by disease at a early age as divine punishment for a parent's sin. And so on. Superstitions too have their origin as a cover for ignorance. I lost my wallet because a black cat crossed my path. My lover left me because Venus was in the wrong house of the zodiac. I won at the roulette table because I was holding my lucky rabbit's foot.

In every case we are faced with a simple reluctance to say: "I don't know." Nothing could be more natural. It is apparently part of the human condition to want explanations, a characteristic we should be proud of. Science is itself an attempt to find a story that satisfies our curiosity about why things happen as they do. What makes the scientific way of knowing unique is a willingness to admit that the cause of an event might be temporarily unknown or even potentially (but let's have a go at it) unknowable.

Traditionally, people have divided explanations into true and false. And *traditionally*, truth is what *we* believe, and falsehood is what *everyone else* believes, if different.

Einstein's remark—as simple as possible, but no simpler—suggests another attitude towards knowledge. He asks us to shave with Ockham's razor, but not cut our throats.

On the one hand, we have *reliable* theories, characterized by the simplicity with which they explain experience. Not upper-case Truths, but provisional truths that work well for the time being and are open to revision when the evidence calls for it. For example, Newton's theory of gravity qualifies as reliable knowledge because of the way a single equation accounts for everything from the motion of planets, to the fall of an apple, to the flow of the tides. With Newton's gravitational law we can predict the return of a comet—Halley's Comet, say—to the day, hundreds of years in advance. *That's* reliable knowledge. The theory of evolution by natural selection explains with almost self-evident simplicity the diversity and interrelatedness of life on Earth as revealed in the fossil record and in the DNA. *That,* too, is reliable knowledge.

That's knowledge as simple as we can make it.

But not simpler. Beyond that, according to Einstein, we must be humble enough to admit our ignorance. With the presumption of knowledge where no reliable knowledge exists goes righteousness. Righteousness breeds pogroms, jihads, and crusades. Righteousness flies airplanes into sky-scrapers and holds children hostage in schools. Righteousness presumes to forcibly impose on others what we think they want or need. If science has given one great gift to the world—greater than the wonders of technology, greater than modern medicine, greater than flights to the moon and planets—it has given us permission not to know everything.

chapter seven

Prayer of the Heart

According to available evidence, the overwhelming majority of people on the planet believe in the efficacy of petitionary prayer—that by some appropriate mix of petition, rite, or sacrifice, the gods (or God) can be cajoled to redirect the normal flow of events in their favor. Never mind that after millennia of prayer not a shred of non-anecdotal evidence exists to affirm divine intervention. Take but one example: For generations, millions of Hindus have prayed for sons—buying prayers, offering sacrifice—yet the ratio of male to female offspring among Hindus is the same as for any other segment of the globe's population. One would think this is pretty convincing evidence for the ineffectiveness of petitionary prayer, but Hindus go right on praying for sons. We continue against all odds to mistake coincidence for evidence—to see, like van Maanen, what we want to see. In recent decades there have been a number of scientific studies—double blind experiments—to look for the efficacy of petitionary prayer in a medical context, the most extensive funded by the Templeton Foundation and managed by Harvard cardiologist Herbert Benson. None have shown positive outcomes.

But surely the creator of the universe has more important things to do than participate in scientific tests of his powers. And for us, more important issues are at stake. To explore them, come with me now to one of Europe's best-known hospitals of two hundred years ago, the Hotel-Dieu in Paris, which claimed to be "the hospital of the kingdom, of Europe, and one might say, of all humanity." Even in the eighteenth century, the Hotel-Dieu had a venerable history. Tradition has it was founded in AD 650 Reliable documentation of the hospital's existence dates from the ninth century. The first enduring buildings went up in 1165. By the eighteenth century, the hospital occupied a large, wedge-shaped block of land on the bank of the Seine, directly in front of Notre Dame cathedral. The description that follows is drawn from Grace Goldin's *Works of Mercy: A Picture History of Hospitals.*

In 1777, the hospital catered to the needs of more than 3,600 patients. Over a door of the hospital were inscribed these words: *C'est icy la Maison de Dieu, et la Porte du Ciel,* "This is the House of God, and the Door to Heaven." The door to heaven, indeed! The death rate at the Hotel-Dieu was one in four. An English visitor reported seeing patients four or five to a bed, some of them dying. Three patients to a bed was the rule; the middle patient's head lay between the feet of the patients to either side. Bed sheets were washed once a month. This work was done by novice nuns, who stood in the polluted waters of the Seine, soaking the sheets, then banging out the crusted soil with a kind of spade. As described by Goldin, this method of doing the laundry was as perilous for the sisters as for the patients. They worked at the river for ten hours a day, beginning at 4 a.m. and ending at 7 p.m., with intervals for prayer and meals. In winter, they had to break the ice, then stand in freezing water. In summer drought they waded into malodorous mud. The novices' long woolen skirts presumably never dried out. Only their faith in God and love of humanity sustained them.

There were no connecting corridors within the hospital; all communication from ward to ward led through other wards, between rows of beds. A ward for madmen was adjacent to one for surgical patients. In Goldin's words, "The howls of the mad took up where the screams of those operated upon left off." A ward for madwomen was a continuation of a maternity ward. Air from the smallpox wards on the fourth floor wafted through the cavernous interconnected buildings, up and down the drafty stairways. It was a rule that convalescents must remain in the hospital for a week after their recovery. In principle, this was to make certain of the cure, but the now-healthy patients were required to spend the time helping in the wards. Their post-recovery probation would as likely as not put them back in bed.

Physicians and nursing staff at the Hotel-Dieu served their clientele bravely and unselfishly, but matters of life and death were left in the hands of God. *Prayers and processions were the primary regimen for effecting cures.* Not much changed in this regard until Florence Nightingale began her hospital reforms in the nineteenth century, emphasizing separation of wards, cleanliness, and appropriate ventilation. Nightingale served her apprenticeship in a Hotel-Dieu-type military hospital in Turkey during the Crimean War. She saw how such hospitals could cause more mortality than the battlefield—seventy-six percent in one six-month period from disease alone. At a different military hospital, built near the end of the war, with a clean water supply, open ventilation, small isolated wards, and adequate

sewage disposal, mortality was only three percent.
Nightingale carried the lesson of the military hospitals
home. Her influence on health care was quickly felt in
Europe and America. The English writer Lytton Strachey
said of Nightingale that she seemed "hardly to distinguish
between the Deity and the Drains," that is, between religious faith and scrupulous elimination of agents of infec-
tion. Only when the Drains—scientific medicine—became
paramount did hospitals enter the modern era.

Still, even in developed countries, the great majority of
us go on praying for medical cures—and no harm in that,
and maybe some marginal mind-body benefit—but few of
us, I suppose, would choose to return to a time before
empirical scientific medicine. One more quick story, anecdotal to be sure, but illustrative nevertheless: In the mid-
1990s, an eye surgeon at a Dublin hospital became
concerned about recurring infections in one of his patients.
An investigation revealed that the source of germs was con-
taminated holy water, with which the patient repeatedly
dabbed her eyes. A subsequent hospital-wide study showed
that non-sterile holy water, brought to patients by their well-
meaning families and friends, was a potentially significant
source of infections.

If petitionary prayer is ineffectual, is there *any* sense in
which an agnostic might pray?

In his journal, the poet Samuel Taylor Coleridge jotted
down what he took to be the five stages of prayer:

> First stage—the pressure of immediate calamities with-
> out earthly aidence makes us cry out to the Invisible.

> Second stage—the dreariness of visible things to a mind
> beginning to be contemplative—horrible Solitude.

> Third stage—Repentance & Regret—& self-inquietude.

Fourth stage—the celestial delectation that follows ardent prayer.

Fifth stage—Self-annihilation—the Soul enters the Holy of Holies.

I can't say I understand what Coleridge meant by all of this—his journal entry stands without explication—but it sounds vaguely like the evolution of prayer in my own life. I would translate Coleridge's stages like this:

First stage—Help!

Second stage—Here I am!

Third stage—Oh my God I am heartily sorry for having offended Thee. . . .

Fourth stage—Gee! followed by, Wow!

Fifth stage—Silent attention.

Does that sound vaguely familiar? I assume my own experience is not unlike that of some others who might be reading this book. For many of us, these stages might correspond to childhood, early adolescence, late adolescence, maturity, and—what shall we call it?—the reflective years. By the way, for those who don't recognize it, my version of stage three is from the Act of Contrition, a prayer we young Roman Catholics mumbled over and over in moments of guilt or fear, in expectation that the recitation of those magic words would win us forgiveness of mortal sin and save us from an eternity in hell. What a relief it was when it finally dawned on me as a young man that the whole panoply of supernaturalism was a sham, and that hell was no more to be feared than heaven longed for. The world suddenly became a place of joyous wonders, and for decades I went on a binge of *gee* and *wow*. Now, as I glide toward the presumed oblivion that is the fate of the agnostic, the *gees* and *wows* have given way to—to silent attention.

There is an ancient tradition of Christian prayer that is open to mystery, yet attuned to God's immanence. It asks for no interventions of a transcendent deity, no response to "Help!" or "Here I am!" It does not beg forgiveness, or assume a listening ear. It begins in the *gee* and *wow*, but turns inward on the self. The Trappist contemplative Thomas Merton described it this way:

> When I am liberated by silence, when I am no longer involved in the measurement of life, but in the living of it, I can discover a form of prayer in which there is effectively no distraction. My whole life becomes a prayer. My whole silence is full of prayer. . . . Let me seek, then, the gift of silence, and poverty, and solitude, where everything I touch is turned into prayer: where the sky is my prayer, the birds are my prayer, the wind in the trees is my prayer, for God is all in all.

Coleridge called it self-annihilation, "the soul entering the Holy of Holies." That may sound a bit over the top, but we know what he's driving at. The emphasis of Coleridge's fifth-stage prayer is not on the isolated self—no "Me, Lord, me"—but rather a co-mingling of self and thing observed. The more fully we grasp the simple *realness* of the world, the more fully are the objects of our attention worthy of gratitude and praise.

The novelist John Updike put it this way: "Ancient religion and modern science agree: We are here to give praise. Or, to slightly tip the expression, to pay attention." It is a happy thought: that religion and science might agree on *something*. But I wonder if there's much common ground. Most religious people will be comfortable with giving praise—singing a *Te Deum*, say—but paying attention to *natural* things might seem peripheral to faith in a supernatural God. Scientists, on the other hand, have raised attention to a high art—and invented telescopes, microscopes, and other instruments to enhance the senses—but the idea of giving praise will sound to many scientists as, well, suspiciously religious. Still, Updike's unorthodox equation of attention and praise has a long history, going back at least to the seventeenth-century philosopher Nicholas Malebranche, who said, "Attention is the highest form of prayer." The art critic John Ruskin wrote: "The greatest thing a human soul ever does in this world is to see something, and to tell what it saw."

Consider this well-known, much-loved eight-line poem by William Carlos Williams:

so much depends
upon

a red wheel
barrow

glazed with rain
water

beside the white
chickens

The poem has been discussed endlessly by critics, but the secret of its appeal remains elusive. Sixteen words. Nursery words. No capitalization. No punctuation. The simplicity of the poem belies its power. Certainly, simplicity is part of the poem's meaning. It affirms something that we all know, even if we cannot put our knowledge into words. Something that exists beyond words, beyond philosophy, beyond science. So much depends. So much depends upon something we can intuit—in silent, jubilant beholding—but not express, not as scientists, not as theologians. Something hidden deep in the exquisite complexity of the world. It is the thing that Thomas Merton draws our attention to in his discussion of prayer, and in particular what he calls "prayer of the heart." He writes: "In the 'prayer of the heart' we seek first of all the deepest ground of our identity in God. We do not reason about dogmas of faith, or 'the mysteries.' We seek

rather to gain a direct existential grasp, a personal experience of the deepest truths of life and faith." We discern this
truth in direct and simple attention to reality, he says.

We need not feel obliged to use the G-word to appreciate
Merton's notion of prayer. Apprehension of a red wheel barrow glazed with rain can be the highest kind of prayer, if, as
the poet suggests, we are aware that so much depends upon
the apprehending. We are struck, rung like a bell, a shudder
down the spine. Color, shape, texture, matter, animation:
red, wheel, glazed, water, chicken. Not a mighty wind that
shatters rocks or tumbles the walls of Jericho. Not Lazarus
waking from the dead. Not a miraculous cure of a terrible
disease. Rather, a red barrow glazed with rain. The prayer of
the heart is not garrulous. It listens in silence, expectant. If,
as so many of the mystics said, the creation is the primary
revelation, then it is when we listen to *what is* that we hear
the voice of God.

chapter eight

The Body Balks Account

*S*oul. What a beautiful and nettlesome word. I've used the word twice in the titles of books: *The Soul of the Night: An Astronomical Pilgrimage*, and *The Virgin and the Mousetrap: Essays in Search of the Soul of Science*. It seems the perfect word to describe the elusive essence of a thing, the thing that is too broad and subtle to be captured by a formula or theorem. The thing that is always the object of a search or a pilgrimage. Once it has been found, it is no longer soul.

Soul is the source of our joy and our anxiety. Joy because it beckons us forward; anxiety because it ever recedes before our grasp, hiding in nature, mask behind mask, veil beneath veil. Anxiety too because of the dualistic burden of the word. "The immaterial essence, animating

principle, or actuating cause of an individual life, usually
thought to be immortal," the dictionary says in its first definition of the word. Immaterial! Immortal! The ghost in the
machine. The fairy sprite that will fly free when bones and
sinews turn to dust.

We know how Walt Whitman regarded the soul, how he
spelled it out in his poem *I Sing the Body Electric*—

> . . . Head, neck, hair, ears, drop and tympan of the ears,
> Eyes, eye-fringes, iris of the eye, eyebrows, and the waking
>   and sleeping of the lids,
> Mouth, tongue, lips, teeth, roof of the mouth, jaws, and the
>   jaw hinges
> . . . The lung-sponges, the stomach-sac, the bowels sweet and
>   clean
> . . . The womb, the teats, nipples, breast-milk, tears, laughter,
>   weeping, love-looks, love-perturbations and risings
> . . . The thin red jellies within you or within me, the bones
>   and the marrow in the bones . . .

to merely dip into his exuberant parsings of the flesh. "Oh I
say now these are the soul!" he enthuses.

Yes. It is enough. One might spend a lifetime with a
person—with a catalog of what Whitman calls the "parts and
poems of the body"—and still not know her soul. Material?
Why not? What a thing is matter! In the formulations of contemporary physics, matter is all vibration, resonance, and
inexhaustible potentialities, a music of the cosmos. If this is
matter, who needs the immaterial? Who requires a ghost in
the machine when the machine itself is a thing of such infinite surprise? The greatest miracle is as close as my next
breath.

"The true mystery of the world is the visible, not the
invisible," said Oscar Wilde. And indeed the smallest insect
is more worthy of our astonishment than a thousand choirs
of angels. The buzzing business of a single cell is more
infused with eternity than any disembodied soul. Even as I

write, a flurry of activity is going on in every cell of my body. Tiny protein-based "motors" crawl along the strands of DNA, transcribing the code into single-strand RNA molecules, which in turn provide the templates for building the many proteins that are my body's warp and weft. Other proteins help pack DNA neatly into the nuclei of cells and maintain the tidy chromosome structures. Still other protein-based "motors" are busily at work untying knots that form in DNA as it is unpacked in the nucleus of a cell and copied during cell division. Others are in charge of quality control, checking for accuracy and repairing errors. Working, spinning, ceaselessly weaving, winding, unwinding, patching, repairing—each cell like a bustling factory of a thousand workers. A trillion cells in my body humming with the business of life.

What a thing it is to think of ourselves as manifestations of this magnificent molecular machinery, ceaselessly animating the world with sensation, emotion, intelligence. To say that it is all chemistry doesn't demean life; rather, it suggests that the fabric of the world is charged with potentialities of a most spectacular sort. Forget all that other stuff—the angels, the auras, the disembodied souls. *Embodied* soul is what really matters.

The philosopher Rene Descartes insisted that body and soul are separate things. "I think, therefore I am," he famously said. His "am" was not flesh and bone. Science refutes Descartes. "I am, therefore I think," is closer to the modern view. The soul *as a thing separate from the body* has been hunted to its lair. The lair is empty. Biology and neuroscience have not found the slightest evidence that a human self can exist independently of the body—not even a hint of body-soul dualism. Whatever the soul is, it is inextricably wrapped in flesh. We are, for better or worse, thinking meat.

So what, then, is a *self?*

We might begin our search for self in the trillions of cells that make up our bodies, which share the same genes. Forensic scientists can identify the perpetrator of a crime from a single hair or drop of semen. To the DNA scientist, a flake of my skin is recognizably me. DNA, like fingerprints or a face, can get us convicted in a court of law.

A second approach to self is embedded in the human immune system. Our bodies have astonishingly complex defenses against non-self invaders that can cause us harm. If it weren't for our immune systems, non-self pathogens and parasites might quickly destroy us. How the body recognizes *threatening* non-self (germs, snake venom) from *harmless* non-self (food, fetus) is one of the most intriguing problems being investigated by science today, and one of paramount importance to medicine. The body knows its own.

Of course, none of this is what we usually mean by a self when we say "I love you," "I'm depressed," "I stubbed my toe," or "You deceive yourself." Personal pronouns assume a self that is more than genetics or immunology. But even this conscious self—this tangle of remembered experience—is embedded in collections of interacting neurons, as brain studies make crystal clear.

The nervous systems of higher animals presumably evolved out of the need for central control of the body's many organs—heart, lungs, viscera, liver, adrenal medulla. Clearly, any system capable of coordinating a bodywide response to danger, or even to coordinate the need for rest and digestion, has a high survival value and will be favored by natural selection. Eventually, evolving nervous systems gave rise to the human brain and self-awareness. Is self-awareness what constitutes a self? Self-awareness can be altered by psychoactive drugs, electrical stimulation, political or religious propaganda, even advertising. Is the person who has been brainwashed to be a suicide bomber acting as his true self?

As the creature with the most complex nervous system, we humans like to think of ourselves as somehow qualitatively different from other animals; thus our affection for the idea of a uniquely disembodied soul. We like to imagine that our selfhood can float free of our physical bodies. But everything we have learned about the human self—from genetics, immunology, neurobiology, and reproductive science—confirms that our selfhood is only the most elaborate of evolution's many levels of cellular organization. To the religious naturalist's way of thinking, this does not lower our stature in the universe, but rather makes us part and parcel of the greatest miracle of all—life's grand thumbing-of-its-nose at nature's law of entropy, which requires the universe to eventually grind every complexity to dust.

Many of us were raised to believe in a self that only temporarily resides in a physical frame. The soul is there at the beginning, we were told, fully formed in the fertilized egg. It survives the body's death and lives forever. This idea of an immaterial, immortal self is perhaps the most cherished of human beliefs. We cling to it. We desperately want it to be true. But not a whit of empirical evidence confirms its existence. No matter. I look at the trillions of interacting cells that are my body, the webs of flickering neurons that are my consciousness, and I see a self vastly more majestic than the paltry soul illustrated in my grade-school catechism as a white circle besmirched with sin. The more I learn about the machinery of life and consciousness, the more profoundly miraculous the self becomes. We are earth, air, fire, and water made conscious. The self comes into existence slowly as cells divide, multiply, and specialize, guided by the DNA, organized by experience. When the organization of cells disintegrates, the self is gone. If to have a soul means anything at all, it means to be confident in our specialness, our uniqueness, our individual significance in the unfolding cosmos. It means to believe that every human life is precious and capable of ennobling the universe.

The Judeo-Christian scriptures tell us that God created the first human being out of the slime of the earth, breathed life into his creation and pronounced it good. The myth is consistent with our current understanding of the nature of the soul. According to the best contemporary science, we are quite literally animated slime. Now we must relearn to think ourselves "good."

A few years ago, *60 Minutes* did a story on a twelve-year-old musical prodigy named Jay Greenberg. Jay had been composing music since he was two, and on the evidence of the televised examples his compositions are of a professional quality. As the program was broadcast, he was studying at Juilliard in New York, where his teachers compared him to Mozart. More recently, *60 Minutes* did a follow-up program highlighting Jay's continuing success.

"It's as if the unconscious mind is giving orders at the speed of light," said Jay, in the first program. "You know, I mean, so I just hear it as if it were a smooth performance of a work that is already written, when it isn't." Jay writes down what he hears, right out of his head, symphonic compositions for entire orchestras, with no revisions. Sometimes he hears more than one composition at a time. "Multiple channels is what it's been termed," he explained. "That my brain is able to control two or three different musics at the same time—along with the channel of everyday life."

What's going on? Where do such prodigies come from? What's different about their brains? It would be interesting to have a PET scan of Jay's brain as it was humming with music.

Some people have extraordinary gifts for music, mathematics, feats of memory, calculation. It's not the size of their brains that is relevant, although certain parts of the brain may be hyperdeveloped. It may have something to do with the sensitivity of synaptic connections between neurons—more neurons are firing, faster, with greater coordination. But no one is certain. Maybe we will never understand the brain completely for the simple reason that consciousness is as complex as the cognitive instrument we have been given to understand it.

The human brain contains about 100 billion neurons, or brain cells. Each neuron has a central body and about 1000 or so tendrils reaching out towards other neurons, almost touching, like the fingertips of God and Adam in the famous painting by Michelangelo. The connections between tendrils are called synapses. There are about 100 trillion synapses in the brain. Each connection can be in one of about 10 different levels of activity. The number of possible states for the brain is 10 raised to the 100 trillionth power, a number greater than the number of particles in the universe. There is not yet a computer on Earth remotely as complex as a human brain. Which is not to say that computers can't do some things faster and better than brains. Complexity isn't everything. Brains have more to do than computers.

My guess is that what makes a prodigy is the right chemicals in the right concentration at the right places to create the right webs of neurons—which says nothing but the obvious. Whatever makes Jay Greenberg unique, he was born that way. It was in his genes, some particular expression of recessive tendencies. Mozarts are born, not made. But chemistry is chemistry. As we learn more about the chemistry of the brain it will be possible to enhance memory, creativity, mood, alertness, self-image, spirituality. It's already happening. It fact, it's been happening since the dawn of time. Alcohol, coffee, chocolate, peyote, meditation, physical rigors: all have been used to modify and enhance consciousness. What is new are designer drugs tailored for specific purposes, with minimal side effects. How society will deal with the neurochemical revolution remains to be seen. It was one thing when the self was thought to be a spirit that could be touched by God alone; now we know that the self is as much a part of the material world as the chair I am sitting on. If you are suffering from Parkinson's disease, or have a chronically depressed child, you will no doubt welcome the new chemical technology. But what about pills that give you an edge in school or on the job? Or pills to make your child better at math or art?

Descartes was wrong. We are not body and soul. We are body. We are colonies of cells who make music, write poems, remember experiences, invent gods, love, hate, build cathedrals, go to war. Most mysteriously of all, we are self-aware. Each of us is a chemistry set that *knows* it is a chemistry set—a chemistry set unlike any other. We may not like to think of our souls as tangled webs of 100 trillion electrochemical connections, each one mediating in some infinitesimal way our interaction with the world. But we better come to terms with it soon if we are going to negotiate the excruciating moral dilemmas that will confront us in the near future. Jay Greenberg doesn't need to reflect on why he is a prodigy; the music just plays in his head. There is a music of sorts playing in each of our heads. It is called the self.

And what of freedom? If our selves are electrochemical machines, in what sense are we free? Art, literature, philosophy, religion are all predicated on the notion that we are free moral agents, able to choose. If we are merely a bunch a flickering synapses, where is the grandeur of the human adventure? Why be a saint rather than a sinner?

I write these words on an island in the central Bahamas. All afternoon I have been watching a pair of hummingbirds play about our porch. They live somewhere nearby, although I haven't found their nest. They are attracted to our hummingbird feeder, which we keep full of sugar water. What perfect little machines they are! No other bird can perform their tricks of flight—flying backwards, hovering in place. Zip. Zip. From perch to perch in a blur of iridescence.

If you want a symbol of freedom, the hummingbird is it. Exuberant. Unpredictable. A streak of pure fun. It is the *speed*, of course, that gives the impression of perfect spontaneity. The bird can perform a dozen intricate maneuvers more quickly than I can turn my head. Is the hummingbird's apparent freedom illusory, a biochemically determined response to stimuli from the environment? Or is the hummingbird's flight what it seems to be, willful and unpredictable? If I can answer that question, I will be learning as much about myself as about the hummingbird.

So I watch. And I consider what I know of biochemistry.

The hummingbird is awash in signals from its environment—visual, olfactory, auditory, and tactile cues that it processes and responds to with lightning speed. How does it do it? Proteins, mostly. Every cell of the hummingbird's body is a buzzing conversation of proteins, each protein a chain of hundreds of amino acids folded into a complex shape like a piece of a three-dimensional jigsaw puzzle. Shapes as various as the words of a human vocabulary.

An odor molecule from a blossom, for example, binds to a protein receptor on a cell membrane of the hummingbird's olfactory organ—like a jigsaw-puzzle piece with its neighbor. This causes the receptor molecule to change that part of its shape that extends inside the cell. Another protein now binds with the new configuration of the receptor, and changes its own shape. And so on, in a sequence of shapeshifting and binding—called a signal-transduction cascade—until the hummingbird's brain "experiences" the odor.

Now appropriate signals must be sent from the brain to the body—ion flows established along neural axons, synapses activated. Wing muscles must respond to direct the hummingbird to the source of nourishment. Tens of thousands of proteins in a myriad of cells talk to each other, each protein genetically prefigured by the hummingbird's DNA to carry on its conversation in a particular part of the body. All of this happens continuously, and so quickly that to my eye the bird's movements are a blur.

Molecular biologists have pretty much solved the problem of how genes make proteins. They are now embarked upon the far more challenging task of deciphering the language of proteins—compiling the dictionary of shapes and the grammar of shapeshifting that lets the hummingbird respond to signals from its environment. There is much left to learn. But this much is clear: There is no ghost in the machine, no hummingbird pilot making moment by moment decisions out of the whiffy stuff of spirit. Every detail of the hummingbird's apparently willful flight is biochemistry.

How much of this applies to my own actions? All of it.

Between myself and the hummingbird there is a difference of *complexity*, but not of *kind*; this is the firm conclusion of contemporary biology, and one of the most important scientific discoveries of the twentieth century. The book of *human* freedom may be *The Complete Works of Shakespeare* compared to the hummingbird's *The Tale of Peter Rabbit*, but the chemical vocabulary and grammar are the same.

Of course, complexity is not without consequence. As we have seen, the human brain contains about 100 billion neurons and each neuron has approximately 1000 synaptic contacts with other neurons, a web of interconnectivity exceeding that of any other creature. If we humans have assumed the role of lords of nature, it is because of the unparalleled tangle of neurons that sits atop our spines. The brain of a simple organism like a worm is hardwired; that is, the neural connections are genetically determined and pretty much the same from worm to worm. It is difficult to speak of a worm's *self*. By contrast, the brains of more complex animals are partly hardwired by genes and partly wire themselves under the influence of experience. As a human brain develops, cells move to locations that are only loosely specified by genes. The migration of any particular cell is dependent upon the cells it moves past and by local hormones those cells secrete, which in turn depend upon an individual's past experience. Every human brain is continuously engaged in the construction of a self. Most of this chemical commerce takes place unconsciously, but our conscious brains are alert to some mental states. As biologist Ursula Goodenough writes: "We are spectators to our own awareness." It is difficult to say to what extent we share this characteristic with other species. Self-awareness appears to have originated with the great apes. Certainly, it has its most spectacular development in *homo sapiens*. But to reiterate: Between the worm, the hummingbird, and the human there is a biochemical continuum, no difference that is not a consequence of neuronal complexity.

What does this mean about human freedom? If we are self-programming biochemical machines in interaction with our environments, in what sense can we be said to be free? What happens to "free will"?

Trying to escape the bugaboo of determinism, some commentators—such as the mathematical physicist Roger Penrose—have looked for the source of human freedom in quantum indeterminacy, the intrinsic stochastic skitter of subatomic particles. But there is no evidence that quantum randomness plays any role in biochemical reactions. Which is just as well, since few of us want to think our much-vaunted freedom is merely quantum noise.

A more satisfying place to look for free will is in what is sometimes called chaos theory. In sufficiently complex systems with many feedback loops—the global economy, the weather, the human nervous system—small perturbations can lead to unpredictable large-scale consequences, though every part of the system is individually deterministic. This has sometimes been called—somewhat facetiously—the butterfly effect: a butterfly flaps its wings in China and triggers a cascade of events that results in a snowstorm in Chicago. Chaos theory has taught us that determinism does not imply predictability. An example: Photons of light and odor molecules from a piece of candy stimulate neurons in my optical and olfactory organs. Signal-transduction cascades inform my brain. *Mmm, candy!* Do I pick up the nougat? Do I put it in my mouth? My action depends not only upon the external stimuli and my genetically inborn taste for sweets, but also upon prior experiences and anticipations of future consequences as recorded in the soft-wired sections of my brain. I pick up the candy or I do not, depending upon a hugely complex—and to an outside observer *unpredictable*—conversation of molecules. This is not what traditional philosophers meant by free will, *but is indistinguishable from what traditional philosophers meant by free will.* If it walks like a duck, and quacks like a duck, it's a duck.

When all is said and done, free will is a social construct, not a scientific hypothesis. Humans long ago discovered that living peaceably in groups required a notion of individual responsibility. Responsibility implies freedom. In contemporary society, it is the judicial system that ultimately decides to what extent our actions are "free." The defense "my genes made me do it" has been found wanting by the courts. Impaired mental competence stands. Both assertions of diminished responsibility are at root biochemical. Science delves; society negotiates responsibility.

I watch the hummingbirds at the feeder. Their hearts beat ten times faster than a human's. They have the highest metabolic rate of any animal, a dozen times higher than a pigeon, a hundred times higher than an elephant. Hummingbirds live at the edge of what is biologically possible, and it's *that,* the fierce intenseness of their aliveness, that makes them appear so exuberantly free. But there are no metaphysical pilots in these little flying machines. The *machines* are the pilots. You give me carbon, oxygen, hydrogen, nitrogen, and a few billion years of evolution, and I'll give you a bird that burns like a luminous flame. The miracle of the hummingbird's freedom was built into the universe from the first moment of creation.

In his marvelous collection of essays on the surgeon's art, the surgeon Richard Selzer tells us that it is the "exact location of the soul" that he seeks as a writer. For thousands of years theologians and philosophers sought to identify the organ of the body that is the residence for our souls, our higher selves. Is it the heart? The brain? Or—as certain ancients claimed—the liver? Medicine is the offshoot of religion, and physicians such as Selzer still pursue the seat of our humanity. But they are no longer so naive as to believe that the soul sits curled up in a cavity of the heart or a lobe of the liver, like a butterfly in a chrysalis, awaiting revelation by the surgeon's knife. Surgeon's have cut away at the body for thousand of years without discovering the seat of the soul. The conclusion is inescapable: The soul must be discerned in the *totality* of the body's animated organs, most especially the brain, and their interaction with the environment. It is less likely to be revealed by the parings of a scalpel than by the writer's art.

Why does a surgeon such as Selzer write? He answers: "It is to search for some meaning in the ritual of surgery, which is at once murderous, painful, healing, and full of love." And what does the surgeon find among the blood and gore? "That man is not ugly, but that he is Beauty itself."

More than three centuries ago, Pascal said: "Man considering himself is the great prodigy of nature. For he cannot conceive what his body is, even less what his spirit is, and least of all how body can be united with spirit." Pascal lived at the dawn of the scientific era, but his words still ring true. We have sent spacecraft to the planets. We have listened to signals from the dawn of time. We have unraveled the mystery of starlight. We can even conceive what the body is. But the deeper human mystery remains: What is the spirit, and how is it united with body? The discovery that our spirits are inextricably linked to electrochemical processes does not diminish our true selves. We still have histories, tell stories, make art. We love, we cry, we respond with awe to the marvelous machinery of cognition. We act as if we were free, and in every respect that matters we are. When necessary, we arm ourselves chemically against the devils of mental illness.

Many of us seem to believe that anything we can understand cannot be worth much, and therefore—most especially— we resist the scientific understanding of self. But the ability to know is the measure of our human uniqueness, the thing that distinguishes us from the other animals. Understanding the machinery of the spirit does not mean that we will ever encompass with our science the rich detail of an individual human life, or the infinitude of ways by which a human brain interacts with the world. Science is a map of the world; it is not the world itself. Nature loves to hide, said Heraclitus, those thousands of years ago. He also said: "You could not discover the limits of soul, not even if you traveled down every road. Such is the depth of its form."

chapter nine

Connected
All the Way
Down

Francis Crick, the codiscoverer of the DNA double helix, writes in his book *The Astonishing Hypothesis*: "To understand ourselves, we must understand how nerve cells behave and how they interact." The "astonishing hypothesis" of Crick's title is simply that we are biochemical machines. Well, perhaps "machines" is not the right word, because no machine yet invented is remotely as complex as the human body. Even a single human cell—this one, here at my fingertip, one of billions, too small to see with the naked eye—makes a Boeing Dreamliner, say, look like a child's toy.

Consider for a moment the little worm *Caenorhabditis elegans* that lives in soil and eats bacteria and is so beloved by developmental biologists. It has only 959 cells in its body,

exactly. Yet *C. elegans* has a primitive sort of brain and a
nervous system that lets it respond to taste, touch, and
smell. It produces eggs and sperm. It grows old and dies. A
fairly sophisticated life for a creature as small as this letter *i*.
The worm's genetic code has been sequenced, approximately 18,000 genes on six chromosomes. Those 18,000 genes
contain all the information necessary for making a worm,
starting with a fertilized egg.

Humans are rather more complicated. Our bodies are
made of trillions of cells, vastly more than the worm's 959.
Yet our genome does not contain a proportionately greater
number of genes. Geneticists currently suppose that we
make do with only about twice as many genes as *C. elegans*.
Obviously, genes are not related to a body in the same way
as an engineer's blueprint is related to a machine. The
genome is not so much a plan of the future organism as it is
a set of instructions for how cells should develop in interaction with their environment. Genes spin off proteins. The
proteins are like craftsmen who build a house without a
blueprint.

Can thirty or forty thousand genes spin out a human
brain, then wire that brain as the organism interacts with its
environment? Yes, say neuroscientists, and that is Crick's
"astonishing hypothesis." Our tendency is to reject this
information, because we like to think we are *more* than biochemistry, that our destiny is to fly free of the physical self.
But don't bet on it. Developmental biologists have pretty
much figured out exactly how *C. elegans* constructs a "self,"
such as it is. The human problem is much more difficult,
but the broad outline for how it happens is in place.

A fertilized egg splits, then again and again. Two, four,
eight, sixteen, eventually trillions of cells. Some cells
become liver. Some backbone. Some skin. A hundred billion
cells become the brain. Each brain neuron has a central
body flanged on one side by long tendrils called axons that

carry signals away from the cell, and on the other side by treelike dendrites that conduct inbound signals. Each neuron reaches out to almost touch a thousand other neurons, axons, and dendrites. As the brain develops in the growing embryo, cells divide, differentiate, migrate. Some die by plan. We are born knowing some things—how to breath, how to suckle, how to cry. But the newborn is not yet the self it will eventually become. More wiring must take place as the brain interacts through the senses with the environment. At the end of each axon are wiggly fingerlike protuberances called growth cones that move about like little animals trailing their axon wiring behind them, hunting in the dark for their final destination, taking in new information as they go, wriggling, fingering, searching, connecting. Building memories. Learning. Making a self. In all of this the genes are in control. By inactivating certain genes in fruitflies, geneticists can redirect the patterns of neural wiring. If our minds are more complex than other animals, it is because we have more neurons and more ways of using genes to connect neurons one to the other.

Are we captives of our genes? Is our destiny written in the language of the DNA? To a certain extent, yes. I was destined from the beginning to be a white Caucasian male, to have black hair and brown eyes, to lose most of my hair in middle age. I was born to be adept at mathematics and lousy at foreign languages. But my genes did not insist that I be the person I am today. I have been making choices since the day I was born, and those growth cones wriggling in the dark responded. For all intents and purposes, I can freely decide what sentence I will write next, and my brain rewires itself accordingly. What we call free will is the unpredictable product of almost infinite electrochemical complexity, but that makes us no less free. Astonishing? Oh, yes, astonishing indeed. But not unbelievable.

What about that part of us that reaches out for God, that longs to see the Mystery bare, not through a glass darkly but face to face? Surely an itch for God is not in our genes. Surely the longing for divinity is more than an electrochemical firestorm in our neurons. An itch for God appears to be universal among humans. In the course of history, humans have invented tens of thousands of religions, many of which are assumed by their adherents to be the divinely-revealed True Faith. Atheism has always been something of an anomaly, and even the word "atheism" has God lurking within it.

Nearly a century ago the American psychologist William James set out to account for the universality of faith in *The Varieties of Religious Experience,* a book that retains a lively presence on college reading lists. James believed that psychological experiences, rather than the tenets or practices of particular faiths, are the essence of the religious life. Behind the warring gods and formulas of the various faiths he sought "states of consciousness" shared by all people. We sense there is something wrong about things as they naturally stand, he wrote, and we are saved from that wrongness by making proper connection with higher powers.

The big question, which James was unable to answer, is whether these universal "states of consciousness" are innate or culturally transmitted. Nature or nurture? Genes or memes?

Genes, of course, are DNA sequences that reside in every cell of our bodies, and are passed largely intact from generation to generation by sexual reproduction. Genes shape our bodies and some behaviors. Memes—a coinage of the biologist Richard Dawkins—are self-replicating units of culture, ideas or concepts passed from one individual to another through writing, speech, ritual, and imitation. Memes can be as trivial as jump-rope rhymes, or as profound as a full-blown theology.

Geneticist Dean Hamer of the National Institutes of Health thinks he has the first proof that some part of religion behavior is innate. He spells out his ideas in *The God Gene: How Faith is Hardwired into Our Genes*, a book that was featured on the cover of *Time* magazine and turned quite a few heads in bookstores. Hamer claims to have confirmed what James suspected: Although the forms and practices of religion are memetic, a tendency towards religious faith is in our genes. That is, we acquire our particular religious beliefs culturally, but we are born with an itch for the transcendent.

Both conclusions can be something of an affront to those who believe that religious faith and practice are responses to supernatural revelation. If you believe you have a direct line to God, you will not be pleased to discover that faith is an accident of nature or nurture. But Hamer, like James before him, professes to leave the existence or nonexistence of a supernatural being out of his discussion. "This is a book about why humans believe," he writes, somewhat disingenuously, "not whether those beliefs are true."

The gist of Hamer's argument is this: He has identified a gene that correlates with a personality trait called *self-transcendence,* as measured on a standard test called a "Temperament and Character Inventory." Self-transcendence is a term used by psychologists to describe spiritual feelings that are independent of traditional religion. It is not based on belief in God, frequency of prayer, or any other conventional religious practice. Self-transcendent people are self-forgetful, and tend to see everything, including themselves, as part of one great totality. They have a strong sense of "at-one-ness" with people, places, and things. They are likely to be environmentalists, or active in the fight against poverty, racism, and war. Self-transcendent individuals are mystical. They are fascinated with things that cannot be explained by science. They are creative, but may also be prone to psychosis. In short, they are spiritual, and inclined to belief in God.

Hamer administered the self-transcendence test to a thousand random subjects. He also sequenced DNA samples from the same individuals, looking specifically at nine genes known to code for chemicals involved in brain activity. One variation of one gene showed a statistically significant correlation with high scores on the self-transcendence inventory. The gene codes for a protein called a monoamine transporter, one of a family of chemicals that controls crucial signaling in the brain. The gene is rather prosaically named VMAT2, and the relevant variation is as simple as one chemical tread on the DNA spiral staircase—in the language of the geneticist, a C rather than an A at position 33050 of the human genome. By analogy, this is like changing a single letter in a dozen sets of the *Encyclopedia Britannica*.

Clearly, both the title and subtitle of Hamer's book, while provocative, are somewhat misleading. It is not "the" God gene that he claims to have identified, but "a" God gene. Hamer readily admits that more than one gene, and their expression in interaction with the environment, are likely involved in something as complex as religious behavior. And it is not religious faith that is hardwired into our genes, but rather a single personality trait as measured by a standard psychological inventory. Self-transcendent persons may or may not believe in God. Interestingly, there were no significant differences in scores for self-transcendence among different racial or ethnic categories; like religion, self-transcendence appears to be a universal human trait. Nor was age a factor. However, women scored significantly higher on the test than men, regardless of age, race, or ethnicity.

Can Hamer be right? Can so slight a variation in our DNA incline us towards religion? It is a slim thread to hang a book on, certainly too slim a thread to support the assertion that faith in God is hardwired into our genes. But sturdy ropes are made of twisted threads, and where Hamer has led others will follow. As geneticists explore the newly sequenced human genome, we will surely hear more about links between genes and behaviors, including religious behaviors.

A genetic link to spirituality will come as no surprise to students of evolutionary psychology. Biologists Edward O. Wilson and Richard Dawkins are just two of many prominent scientists who have proposed innate religious behaviors.

Wilson writes: "The predisposition to religious belief is the most complex and powerful force in the human mind and in all probability an ineradicable part of human nature." And there are ample reasons, he notes, why natural selection might have favored such tendencies. For example, stratified and cohesive societies tend to fare best in conflict with their neighbors, says Wilson, and religion provides both hierarchy and cohesion. Even today, most of the conflicts in the world are between groups unified by religious beliefs.

Wilson's supposition assumes that natural selection can favor groups as well as individuals. However, not all biologists believe group selection plays a significant role in evolution. Richard Dawkins has suggested (admittedly without proof) that what has been favored by natural selection is infant credulity. The child who innately respects parental authority ("Don't go in the water or the crocodiles will eat you.") is most likely to survive and reproduce his or her genes. An inborn credulity trait, if it exists, might then be exploited by priests, shamans, or tribal elders as a way of gaining power or strengthening the cohesiveness of the group, says Dawkins.

If evolutionary biologists such as Wilson and Dawkins are right, religion is beneficial to our physical and mental health, which is why "God genes" may have been selected by evolution. Up to now, however, evolutionary biologists have been theorizing in the dark. It is Hamer's contribution to provide the first tentative link between a specific gene and religious behavior.

And what if it's true? What should be our response to the discovery that the behavioral basis of faith is hardwired into our DNA?

Some believers will reasonably suppose that if God wanted us to acknowledge his existence he might logically provide us with an innate predisposition to belief. (Although one might wonder why he would provide the C-version of the VMAT2 gene to some of us, and not to others.) Most believers, I would guess, will say that this "God-gene" business is a tempest in a scientific teapot. They will admit that some degree of self-transcendence may be innate, like a talent for mathematics or music, but deny any relevance to revealed truth. People of faith have traditionally resisted any attempt of "deterministic," "reductionistic," and "materialist" science to see religion as something other than supernaturally inspired. When Hamer first broached the idea of a God gene in an essay for the online magazine *Slate*, the response of believers was quick and overwhelmingly negative, he tells us in the book.

In *The Varieties of Religious Experience*, William James wrote: "The truth is that in the metaphysical and religious sphere, articulate reasons are cogent for us only when our inarticulate feelings of reality have already been impressed in favor of the same conclusion." He did not, of course, have anything to say about genes or brain chemistry as the source of the "inarticulate feelings"—it was too early for that—but he was convinced that an innate propensity towards belief lay behind every great world religion, be it Buddhism or Christianity. "The unreasoned and immediate assurance is the deep thing in us, the reasoned argument is but a surface exhibition," he wrote. Almost a century later, E. O. Wilson agrees that religiosity is innate. In his best-selling book *Consilience*, he writes: "For many the urge to believe in transcendental existence and immortality is overpowering.

Transcendentalism, especially when reinforced by religious faith, is psychically full and rich; it feels somehow right." A thoroughgoing empiricist himself, Wilson readily concedes that transcendentalism will always trump empiricism. "The human mind evolved to believe in the gods," he says; "it did not evolve to believe in biology."

And if it turns out that religion has its origins in brain chemistry, is that necessarily a bad thing? Self-transcendence—identification with something greater than ourselves—is an aspect of religion we can all admire. Even a secular humanist such as Wilson acknowledges that religion is largely beneficent. "It nourishes love, devotion, and, above all, hope. People hunger for the assurance it offers," he writes. "I can think of nothing more emotionally compelling than the Christian doctrine that God incarnated himself in testimony of the sacredness of all human life, even of the slave, and that he died and rose again in promise of eternal life for everyone." Certainly, the Sermon on the Mount lays out a body of self-transcendent memes we can all profitably live by. And if ever there was a meme that deserved wide circulation it is: "Do unto others as you would have them do unto you." Unfortunately, other of our religious memes have given us inquisitions, crusades, pogroms, and jihads. "Oh how we hate one another," said Cardinal Newman, "for the love of God." Happy the world in which a VMAT2 C-variant inclines us away from self-aggrandizement.

Dean Hamer is cautious in suggesting the theological implications of his research. However, as a biologist and geneticist, he offers three insights into the perceived conflict between science and faith. First, science can tell us whether there are God genes, he says, but not whether there is a God. Spiritual experiences, like all experiences, must be interpreted by our biologically constructed brains. Second, spiritual enlightenment takes practice, he says, and self-transcendence can be enhanced by such traditional practices as meditation, psychoactive drugs, or self-imposed physical rigors. What we do with our spiritual genes is up to us. Lastly, and most important in Hamer's view, is the difference between spirituality and religion, a point made equally strongly by William James. Some part of spirituality may be an inherited ebb and flow of monoamines in the brain, but the forms and practices of religion are cultural, passed from one person to another by learning or imitation.

It remains to be seen whether Hamer's research bears up to further scientific scrutiny, and whether further research will reveal even more of the biochemical basis for spirituality. If religious behavior is part of our human nature, it is easy to understand why religions are universal, and why belief in God and personal immortality are not going away any time soon.

And what of the war between science and faith? It is likely to continue, perhaps become even more strident as science learns more about how the mind works.

By definition, science cannot *prove* the existence or nonexistence of the supernatural. What science can do is show that there is no evidence, other than anecdotal, for immaterial souls, miracles, or answered prayers. Ockham's razor has been a powerful tool for acquiring reliable knowledge of the world, and scientists generally are reluctant to multiply hypotheses beyond what is necessary to explain the phenomena. Although scientists as a group are much less likely to believe in God and the supernatural than the general population, in my experience they are no less "spiritual." Microbiologist Ursula Goodenough, for example, is not a theist, but considers herself deeply religious. In her wonderful book, *The Sacred Depths of Nature*, she reminds us that the word religion derives from the Latin *religio*, to bind together again. She writes:

> We have throughout the ages sought connection with higher powers in the sky or beneath the earth, or with ancestors living in some other realm. We have also sought, and found, religious fellowship with one another. And now we realize that we are connected to all creatures. Not just in food chains or ecological equilibria. We share a common ancestor. . . . We share evolutionary constraints and possibilities. We are connected all the way down.

In revealing the universe of the galaxies and the DNA, science opens our eyes to a creative power of far greater majesty and mystery than the Olympian divinities of our ancestors, and many of us would like to see theologians adapt their memes to the new evolutionary story of the universe. As Wilson writes in *Consilience*: "The spirits our ancestors knew intimately first fled the rocks and trees, then the distant mountains. Now they are in the stars, where their final extinction is possible. But we cannot live without them. People need a sacred narrative." Can such a narrative be found, one that is not in conflict with science? Wilson thinks so. The true evolutionary epic, retold as poetry, is as intrinsically ennobling as any religious epic, he says. And religious naturalists agree. We stand ready to embrace the evolutionary story of creation as a satisfying ground for spirituality.

Thomas Berry, cultural historian, environmentalist, and Roman Catholic priest, urges us to assimilate the scientific story of creation—what he calls the New Story—into our religious and prayerful lives: "The universe, the solar system, and the planet earth in themselves and in their evolutionary emergence constitute for the human community the primary revelation of that ultimate mystery whence all things emerge into being." The forms of religious belief that guided us in the past are inadequate to energize our future, he says. The ancient Christian creation story has functioned well in its institutional and moral efficiency, but it is no longer the integral story of the Earth and mankind, the story by which we live our daily, highly technological lives. Further, the old story is a sectarian story, focused on the personality of the Savior. It has become, he says, "dysfunctional." For Berry, the spiritual significance of the New Story, the scientific story, is this: The universe is a unity— an interacting, evolving, and genetically-related community of beings bound together inseparably in space and time. Our responsibilities to each other and to all of creation are implicit in this unity. Each of us is profoundly implicated in the functioning and fate of every other being on the planet, and ultimately, perhaps, throughout the universe.

Science cannot resolve the conflict between science and faith; science must go wherever it is led by the empirical method, peeling away the veils in which nature hides. If the conflict between science and religion is to be resolved, it is up to persons of faith to modify their memes, and indeed this has been happening since the beginning of human history. Most Catholics, for example—to refer to my own birth tradition—no longer talk about banishing unbaptized babies to Limbo or believe Genesis offers a literal account of creation. The Index of Forbidden Books is gone, Galileo has been rehabilitated, and Catholic institutions of higher education excel as centers of scientific research. Even in my lifetime a significant measure of accommodation has occurred between science and faith. But much more magical and superstitious thinking remains to be stripped away.

And when all the magical thinking is gone, what are we left with? With plenty. Faith communities *at their best* add immeasurably to the storehouse of human well-being. Works of charity, celebration of the ineffable Mystery of the world, rites of passage, ethical principles: all of these have no conflict with science. And surely we can learn to celebrate the wisdom of our respective faith traditions without seeking to impose our traditions on others.

But past experience suggests that reconciling science and faith will be slow, with a hefty dose of fundamentalist reaction along the way. Genes and memes—those primordial forces—are sturdily resilient.

When God Is Gone, Everything Is Holy

Spry little x, with its feet planted firmly on the ground and its arms uplifted in surprise, is our emissary to the unknown. Rene Descartes, in his book on geometry in 1637, first used x to stand for the undetermined variable in mathematical equations. Since then we have trotted out x as a place keeper when the true identity of a thing is unknown: the mysterious Mr. X, the creature from Planet X, secret ingredient X. When in 1895 Wilhelm Konrad Roentgen discovered penetrating radiations of an unknown nature, he called them X-rays. We love our mysteries. News of Roentgen's discovery spread like wildfire. "Wondrous rays." "See the bones in your hand." "Count the coins within your purse." Now Roentgen's magical rays have become

commonplace. So we turn to other sources of mystery.
Black hole X-1. Television's *X-Files*. X marks the spot.

Which brings me by a curious Cartesian arc to . . . to God.

As I write, two books that do their best to reduce God *ad
absurdum* are being talked about everywhere: Richard
Dawkins's *The God Delusion* and Sam Harris's *The End of
Faith*. The authors go at religion like B-movie slashers
armed with Ockham's razor, and by the time they are fin-
ished there is not much left but the gory shreds of miracles
and superstitions. I enjoyed both performances. God had it
coming. But I won't go where Dawkins and Harris would
like to take me. Something is amiss with their militant,
slash-and-burn atheism. If I can switch metaphors—and
turn the new one on its ear—Dawkins and Harris throw out
the bath water with the baby.

In my inverted cliché, let "the bath water" stand for the
mind-stretching, jaw-dropping, in-your-face wonder of the
universe itself, the Heraclitean mystery that hides in every
rainbow, every snowflake, every living cell. After all, water,
as much as anything in our environment, is an adequate
symbol for the creative agency that forges atoms in the hot
interiors of stars, weds oxygen to hydrogen, and wets the
Earth with the stuff of life and consciousness—an agency
worthy of attention, reverence, thanksgiving, praise. As for
"the baby," let that represent the cultural accretions that
religious traditions have affixed to the "water" of mystery—
the anthropomorphisms, misplaced pieties, triumphalism,
intolerance toward "infidels," supposed miracles, and supernatural imaginings. Memes without substance.

So, yes, toss out the baby, but save the water.

What about those other scientists who have authored currently popular books—Francis Collins and Owen Gingerich,
for example—Christian theists who opt for (in Stephen Jay
Gould's phrase) "non-overlapping magisteria" of science and
religion; they want the bath water and the baby too. But can
a scientist who is committed to naturalistic explanations

believe in a religion founded on miracles, and if so, how does he reconcile two contradictory ways of knowing? If Collins and Gingerich had been born in China, say, or India, their science would be the same, but their religion would almost certainly be different. Accidents of birth are surely an unreliable guide to truth. Which is why the religious naturalist or scientific agnostic chooses a single magisterium—a natural world that can be known empirically, however imperfectly. At this moment in history, the most reliable way of knowing the natural world is science.

Of all the cultural encrustations of natural religion, the most troublesome has been the notion of a *personal* God, a viral meme that infects—in one way or another—Harris, Dawkins, Collins, and Gingerich, as well as almost everyone else who writes on the subject of science and faith, myself included. God *in our own image.* God invested with human qualities: justice, love, will, desire, jealousy, artifice, and so on—in short, attributes of human personhood. The divinity of the conventional theist is not so much seen through a glass darkly as in a mirror brightly. And what could be more natural? What metaphor is closer to hand than our own self-awareness? Prescientific people invested every tree, brook, and celestial body with personhood. For all of its grandeur and refinement, the modern idea of a transcendent personal deity who acts willfully in the world is only the final manifestation of ancient animism. For the religious agnostic, this is the ultimate idolatry.

The personhood of God is the memetic offspring of human imagination. So, yes, toss it. But retain the waters of refreshment, the beautiful and terrible mystery that soaks creation as water soaks a rag, diminished by any name we give it—the abiding, intuited, Ultimate X.

The scientific atheists (Richard Dawkins and Sam Harris, for example) and the scientific theists (Francis Collins and Owen Gingerich, for example) hammer away at each other. We haven't had such a rousing clash of God-debunkers and God-clingers since the days of Thomas Huxley and Bishop Wilberforce. Meanwhile, those of us in the "nature loves to hide" tradition go quietly on our way, wondering what the fuss is all about. We fully accept the scientific view of the world, and regard as superfluous any appeal to the supernatural. Yet we are not adverse to being called religious. Our response to the natural world is one of reverence and humility in the face of a mystery that transcends empirical knowing—now, certainly, and perhaps forever. "Agnostic" does not do justice to the *celebratory* aspect of our position. Nor does "pantheist" adequately express our sense of what nature hides. "Creation-based spirituality" has a respectable pedigree, although "creation" hints at an anthropomorphic Creator. "Religious naturalism" gets close to the mark.

Whatever we choose to call it, we are part of a tradition that has found expression within all of the major religions of the world. Within the heritage I know best—Roman Catholic Christianity—the tradition has been espoused by voices as various as the fifth-century Celt Pelagius and the twentieth-century scientist/mystic Pierre Teilhard de Chardin. Invariably, religious naturalists within the Catholic tradition have found themselves outside official favor in a Church overwhelmingly defined by a dualistic natural/supernatural neo-Platonism.

If one were looking for a patron saint of religious naturalism *within the Christian tradition,* one could do no better than read the sermons of the thirteenth-century Dominican friar, Meister Eckhart. I first read Eckhart as a young Catholic graduate student in physics, in a red-bound paperback edition that still lurks somewhere in my library. At the time, I had only a vague idea what I was looking for, but I sensed that Eckhart was part of it. Here is the theologian Matthew Fox's account of Eckhart's theology, which I summarize and interpret:

- God's word gives rise to the goodness of creation. Although "word" smacks of anthropomorphism, it is a mistake to think of Eckhart's God as a person "out there" or "wholly other." Divinity is inseparable from nature. There are no dualisms of body/soul, natural/supernatural, matter/spirit. Eckhart's spirituality is an emphatic *acceptance* of creation.

- With Eckhart's *via positiva* there is also a *via negativa*. God is not this and is not that. God is unknown and unnamable, a mystery sensed intuitively as through a glass darkly. Eckhart "prays God to rid me of God" in order to experience more fully the *ineffability* and *unfathomabilty* of creation.

- We are not other than God. We are part of the creation, part of the ineffable. Our eternal life, such as it is, consists in being part—here, now—of life eternal.

- Our spiritual journey is not defined by up/down. We are not asked to despise the body. Our goal is not some otherworldly "higher" life. Spiritual growth moves outward to embrace the cosmos and returns to self. Outward and returning, an endless spiral. "If people lived for a thousand years or even longer," says Eckhart, "they might still gain in love."

- To the extent that we participate in the divine, we are creators, of art, certainly, but also of justice and compassion. Eckhart's Trinity is *being, knowing, doing*. We are not hobbled in our search by Original Sin; on the contrary, we are enabled by

the blessedness of the creation of which we are a
part. Pleasure—bodily, sensual pleasure—is part of
the spiritual experience.

In assessing Eckhart's theological relevance to our own
time, we must take into account the conceptual universe in
which he lived and the spiritual traditions he was heir to,
which were thoroughly medieval. Still, in Eckhart's sermons, we glimpse a tradition of creation spirituality or religious naturalism that stands in stark opposition to the
predominant nature/supernature opposition that has
defined mainstream Christianity at least since the time
of Augustine.

Two things in particular distinguish the Eckhartian tradition from the Augustinian: a unitary rather than dualistic
understanding of the world, and an unwillingness to speak
of God as a person, or, for that matter, to speak of him (her?
it?) at all. Fall/redemption, body/soul, matter/spirit, natu-
ral/supernatural: These distinctions, in the Eckhartian
view, are artificial impediments to a fully joyous spiritual
engagement with the creation. And, it must be said, these
same oppositions are at the root of the current tension
between science and religion. The first step in Eckhartian
spirituality is to say "yes" to creation, withholding nothing,
reserving no part of our heart or mind for a Wholly Other.

Is there any chance that my own tradition of Roman
Catholicism might be reconciled with religious naturalism?
This is a complicated question, fraught with historical rami-
fications. But let me address it here as best I can, as a religious naturalist trained as a scientist. Much of what I have to
say will apply to other faith traditions. The reader can make
the appropriate translations.

I have spent most of my adult life associated within
Catholic higher education, mainly with two institutions—

the University of Notre Dame and Stonehill College—founded and maintained by the Congregation of Holy Cross, a community of brilliant and compassionate men and women dedicated to education. Many of these men were my teachers and friends, and never in forty years in their company did I experience anything but support for my teaching and writing, even as I lapsed from formal communion. The atmosphere in which I worked was tolerant and supportive of diversity.

Both institutions are presently concerned about their Catholic identity. They define themselves as Catholic colleges, and their students are mainly the children of devout or nominally Catholic families. But the faculties are increasingly lay and non-Catholic, and the formal trappings of Catholicism that I experienced as a student at Notre Dame in the 1950s and at Stonehill in the 1960s—prayers before classes, courses in apologetics, teachers with Roman collars, etc.—are no longer much in evidence. A casual visitor to either campus would be hard-pressed to recognize the place as Church-related. Meanwhile, Notre Dame has graduate and undergraduate science programs of the first rank—world-class science that makes no reference to faith traditions—and, as I write, Stonehill is preparing to invest in a splendid new science building, the most ambitious project in the school's history. And there's the rub.

Science and religious faith are the two greatest forces in the world today, and the tension between them is palpable and real. In Catholic higher education, the battle with the *content* of science has been mostly won; the science taught in the best Catholic colleges and universities is identical to that of any of our great secular institutions. But the clash of orthodox theology with the *spirit* of the scientific way of knowing is generally swept under the rug, and the tension will become more acute as scientists learn more about the genetic, chemical, and anthropological origins of religious faith.

Theologically, it's as if the Scientific Revolution never happened. We teach twenty-first-century science in the classroom, and in the chapel we recite a Creed based on neolithic cosmologies. No wonder it is so difficult to find and hire top-notch Catholic scholars; we are asking them to live in two contradictory conceptual worlds at once. Meanwhile, we tell ourselves that there is no contradiction between classroom and chapel because science and faith belong to separate domains. But knowledge is a single domain, and it was the historic triumph of Christian Europe (with significant assists from elsewhere, especially from Hellenic Alexandria) to devise a *unitary* way of knowing—the scientific way of knowing—that is more reliable than tradition or revelation.

Towards the end of the nineteenth century, forward-looking Catholic theologians and philosophers sought to reformulate Catholic doctrine in ways that were consistent with empirical learning, and to undo the long tension between science and faith that stretched back to Galileo—and beyond. This forward-looking movement was condemned as the Modernist heresy, and formally crushed with the 1907 encyclical *Pascendi Dominici Gregis* and "Syllabus Condemning the Errors of the Modernists." The oppressive influence of these documents, together with the stultifying doctrine of papal infallibility promulgated in 1870, rendered serious discussion of the intrinsic conflict of science and Catholic faith-based cosmology mute throughout the twentieth century. *Pascendi Dominici Gregis* is an extraordinary document, the general drift of which can be stated: God has revealed through Holy Scriptures and Apostolic Tradition everything that is necessary to know about God and his relationship to humankind, and men and women must put aside their doubts and humbly accept the immutable truths of faith. "Curiosity by itself, if not prudently regulated, suffices to account for all errors," says the document flatly. And so with a blunt fist, the Church sought to crush the very thing that makes us most majestically human: our questing intelligence.

The conflict at the heart of Catholic education will not be resolved until the effects of the Modernist condemnation are consigned to the trash heap of history. This means that Catholic theologians must *openly* examine the relevance of archaic doctrines to the modern world. Body-soul dualism, personal immortality, heaven and hell, the resurrection, the divinity of the historical Jesus, miracles, Catholic triumphalism: all are in thrall to an understanding of the world that has been scientifically obsolete since the seventeenth century. Also up for examination are the Church's historic paternalism, Jansenism, misogyny, anti-Semitism, and homophobia.

Is it possible that so formidable an institution as the Roman Catholic Church could transform itself so radically? A slim ray of hope can be found in what Catholic tradition calls the *sensus fidelium,* "sense of the faithful." Just as the Spirit supposedly guides the infallible magisterium so that it doesn't propose teachings that would lead the whole Church into error, so the faithful, as a whole, have an instinct or "sense" about when a teaching is—or is not—in harmony with faith. Is it possible that the *sensus fidelium* will shift *Pascendi Dominici Gregis* into well-deserved irrelevance? Traditionalists will respond by quoting Paul: "If Christ did not rise from the dead, then your faith is in vain." Well, yes, and this is the ultimate impediment to radical transformation— and the reason why science and Christian faith are likely to remain at odds. If Jesus did not rise from the dead, then faith that he was identical with the creator of the universe and that he triumphed over death are indeed in vain. But identification with the Jesus of the Sermon on the Mount is not in vain. Identification with the Jesus who suffered and died for what he thought was the good of humankind is not in vain. Identification with the Jesus who embraced sinners, lepers, and the poor is not in vain. Identification with the Jesus who

suffered very human doubt on the cross is not in vain. Nor
does it matter if these events happened as recorded by the
evangelists. That is to say, everything that is good and holy
about Christian tradition depends not a whit upon the two-
thousand-year-old supernaturalist myths that were contrived, perhaps sincerely, by Jesus' admirers and immediate
successors and codified at Nicea.

In place of the spirit and demon-haunted world of our pre-
scientific ancestors, a renewed Church would embrace the
evolving empirical cosmology of the twenty-first century—
what Thomas Berry calls "the New Story." The antagonisms
between science and faith are deeper than they might appear
to be, writes Berry. The older redemptive stories of the Judeo-
Christian tradition simply do not meet the most basic tests of
rational knowing, he says. But the newer, scientific story
of creation has not yet acquired a spiritual aspect: "An integral story has not emerged." It should be part of the mission
of Catholic colleges and universities to help forge the integral
story—to make sacred and holy the world described by science. In a world beset by religious strife, no mission can be
more important to our collective future.

Still, I hear the protest: If we jettison what most
Catholics consider to be the dogmatic core of their faith—
Nicean dogma—what remains to identify our colleges and
universities as uniquely Catholic?

The sacramental and liturgical life of the Church will
survive intact, gracious, and transforming. Human nature
hasn't substantially changed in 10,000 years. We still sense
the world as sacred. We still long for communities of shared
celebration and praise. We still want rites of passage. We still
need the experience of contemplative prayer. We still must
attend again and again to the lesson of the Sermon on the
Mount. Sanctity does not require a supernatural referent for
its definition. Nor does grace.

There is a vast tradition of uniquely Catholic literature,
art, and music that takes us to the heart of the human

search for meaning. Gerard Manley Hopkins, Mary Gordon, Walker Percy, Sigrid Undset, Georges Bernanos, Evelyn Waugh, Flannery O'Connor, Andre Dubus, Graham Greene, Shusaku Endo, and countless other Catholic writers rank with the best the modern age has to offer.

There is a tradition of Catholic social justice that should to be brought to the fore. Catholic religious communities and lay people have made monumental contributions to medicine, education, and service to the poor that can inspire our students to similar selflessness. The modern mystical tradition, exemplified by Thomas Merton, Teilhard de Chardin, and many others, sharpens our perceptions of an intuited quality of the world that resists empirical analysis. The monastic tradition has much to teach us about balancing reflection, work, and learning in our individual lives.

And—most importantly—who better to infuse the scientific way of knowing with a sense of the sacred and respect for human dignity than the Church that stumbled with Galileo? Who better to lead the way into an ecologically healthy future for the planet than the Church that has misdirected so much of its influence and energy in denigrating the material world?

Yes, there can be a glorious mission for Church-related higher education once we understand that we are not prisoners of archaic dogma and neolithic ways of knowing, once we understand that we are in possession of a tradition that is as rich in sacred virtue as it is shameful in human failure. The Modernists tried to lead us out of the wilderness. So did John XXIII. In both instances the Church showed a failure of the will—an unwillingness to define itself in terms of the future rather than the past.

Everything I have said here about Catholicism applies in a greater or lesser extent to other faith traditions.

Will the changes I sketch happen anytime soon? Not likely. Entrenched authoritarian bureaucracies resist transformation, and people everywhere are reluctant to give up traditional beliefs, even as it becomes clear that faith commitments are overwhelmingly determined by accidents of birth. Nevertheless, *de facto* reformation is inevitable. Catholic lay people and communities of professed women and men—especially women, in my experience—are leading the way towards an identity that is defined less by medieval dogma and more by twenty-first-century practice. As one long associated with Catholic higher education and deeply enamored of the best of that tradition, I continue to hope that Catholic educators will resist a relapse into religious fundamentalism and become instead a shining example of the virtues so necessary for our common future—a love for the world as we empirically find it, and a sense that everything in it is holy.

chapter eleven

What Then of God?

Here is a little poem called "Sacrament" by the Canadian poet Alden Nowlan, which I quote in its entirety:

> God, I have sought you as a fox seeks chickens,
> curbing my hunger with cunning.
> The times I have tasted your flesh
> there was no bread and wine between us,
> only night and the wind beating the grass.

Night, wind, grass. And, yes, bread and wine too, although not as symbols of something otherworldly and divine, but as themselves. Bread, wine, candlelight, rain on window glass, thunder somewhere afar off. The early morning coo of the mourning dove. A stone picked up along the path, hard and cool in the hand.

If I am to have a scripture, let it be written in the language of *things*. Concrete, sensual, particular things. This woman that I love. The touch of her skin. This drop of rain on glass. This stone. This God who hides in the interstices of creation, who whispers his revelations as sweet nothings, in the inarticulate language lovers use. The God I seek is not selfish or insistent. He will be found, if he is found at all, by walking through the dark valley. The seeker hardly dares to speak his name for fear that he will disappear at the sound of her voice. The God I seek will come in silence. The essayist Pico Iyer writes, "Silence is the tribute that we pay to holiness; we slip off words when we enter a sacred place, just as we slip off shoes."

Any religion worthy of humankind's future will have these characteristics:

—It will be ecumenical. It will not imagine itself as "truer" than other religions. It will be open and welcoming to best and holiest of all faith traditions.

—It will be ecological. It will take the planet and all of its creatures into its commandment of love.

—It will embrace the scientific story of the world as the most *reliable* cosmology, not necessarily true, but truer than the neolithic alternatives that presently give shape to the world's theologies. It will look for the signature of divinity in the extravagant wonder of the creation itself, not in supposed miracles or exceptions to nature's laws. Ursula Goodenough writes: "The religious naturalist is provisioned with tales of natural emergence that are, to my mind, far more magical than traditional miracles. Emergence is inherent in everything that is alive, allowing our yearning for supernatural miracles to be subsumed by our joy in the countless miracles that surround us." To which I say amen. And amen again.

If I may generalize, there have traditionally been two pathways to God.

The first path—followed by the overwhelming majority of believers—looks for God in exceptional events. In miracles. The stacked crutches at Lourdes. The raising of Lazarus from the dead. Making the blind see. The virgin birth. Answered prayers. There was a time, of course, when *everything* was explained by the interventions of supernatural agencies. The sun was driven across the sky each day by the god Helios in his golden chariot. Comets were divine portents. Plagues were signs of God's displeasure. Every brook, tree, and mountain had its supernatural spirit. Then, in the eastern Mediterranean world during the several centuries before the Christian era, a new way of knowing was invented. Miracles were banished as explanations, the anthropomorphic gods sent packing. Instead, certain curious men and women began to look for *patterns* in natural events, and to express those patterns as predictive laws. After flourishing briefly, especially in Alexandria, this new way of knowing—today we call it science—was overwhelmed by the human predilection for the supernatural, and the great library of Alexandria was destroyed by religious zealots. But the empirical philosophy did not die. It was revived at the time of the Scientific Revolution in the sixteenth and seventeenth centuries and became the basis for modern medicine, technology, and even, some might argue, through its handmaiden the Enlightenment, our political and religious freedoms.

But even now, as we enter the twenty-first century, supernaturalism retains a powerful hold on the human imagination. God's hand is still sought in those things we don't yet fully understand: the big bang, the origin of life, the emergence of self-awareness. This is the God of the gaps. The God of "intelligent design."

Gaps have a way of being filled. We no longer see God's intervening will in the appearance of a comet, or look for divine meaning in the death of a child from disease. I would hate to think that my own faith in God depended upon scientists never figuring out exactly how the blood-clotting protein cascade evolved, or how the flagellum of a bacterium evolved, to mention just two of the so-called "irreducibly complex" aspects of life that are sometimes offered as evidence for intelligent design.

It is easy to understand why the God of the gaps is so popular. By looking for God in our ignorance, we can make him in our own image, call him Father, speak to him as friend, claim a personal relationship, count on his intervention in our lives. It is a consoling thought to think that the creator of the universe—those hundreds of billions of galaxies—has me, yes *me*, as the apple of his eye. Who would not want it to be so?

A second pathway to God looks to the creation as the primary revelation.

Saint Columbanus was typical of the earliest generations of Irish Christians when he wrote: "Who shall examine the secret depths of God? Who shall dare to treat of the eternal source of the universe? Who shall boast of knowing the infinite God, who fills all and surrounds all, who enters into all and passes beyond all, who occupies all and escapes all?" Those who wish to know God, he said, must first review the natural world. This second pathway to God has nothing to fear from science. With the discovery of the universe of the galaxies, the geologic eons, the wonders of evolution, and the dance of the DNA, our eyes are opened to a majesty and a mystery of far greater dimension than the Olympian deities of our ancestors—or of the slightly more abstracted personal God worshipped by most believers today.

Columbanus's God is the God of mystery, the *Deus absconditus* of the mystics, the hidden God who is not this and is not that, who evades all names and metaphors, even the pronouns "who" and "he," Rudolph Otto's *mysterium tremendum et fascinans*. It is not a God with whom we can have a personal relationship or who attends our personal needs. It is a God we approach through the valley of shadow and the dark

night of the soul, who always hides just beyond our reach. We
don't discover this God through bible-thumping televangelists
or the infallible pronouncements of a pope, but through the
explorations of the great spiritual pilgrims—Julian of
Norwich, John of the Cross, Meister Eckhart, Georges
Bernanos, Sigrid Undset, Gerard Manley Hopkins, Simone
Weil, Nikos Kazantzakis, Pierre Teilhard de Chardin, Thomas
Merton, Flannery O'Connor, to name just a few from my
own tradition.

Nikos Kazantzakis's "dread essence beyond logic" is not
diminished by science. Listen again to the Roman Catholic
priest and cultural historian Thomas Berry:

> Today, in the opening years of the twenty-first century,
> we find ourselves in a critical moment when the reli-
> gious traditions need to awaken again to the natural
> world as the primary manifestation of the divine to
> human intelligence. The very nature and purpose of the
> human is to experience this intimate presence that
> comes to us through natural phenomena. Such is the
> purpose of having eyes and ears and feeling sensitivity,
> and all our other senses. We have no inner spiritual
> development without outer experience. Immediately,
> when we see or experience any natural phenomenon,
> when we see a flower, a butterfly, a tree, when we feel
> the evening breeze flow over us or wade in a stream of
> clear water, our natural response is immediate, intuitive,
> transforming, ecstatic. Everywhere we find ourselves
> invaded by the world of the sacred.

It was my habit over my long years of teaching to give a
few favorite students the gift of a book at graduation. The
book I gave most often was Sigrid Undset's Nobel Prize
winning-novel *Kristin Lavransdatter*, a 1200-page saga of
fourteenth-century Norway. I first read the novel in my
twenties, nearly half-a-century ago, in the Charles Archer

translation from the 1920s, and was deeply moved. I read it again recently in Tina Nunnally's more accessible rendering. I am older now than was Kristin when she died of the Black Death. Like Kristin, I have children, grandchildren, and a long marriage. The novel rings with the truth of a life lived and of a lifelong search for God. Surely, part of the reason I so enjoyed the novel as a young man and again recently is that it is intensely Roman Catholic. (I read it the first time upon the recommendation of Notre Dame's new young president Father Ted Hesburgh.) Norway in the early fourteenth century was Catholic, having been brought into the pan-European fold by sainted King Olav in the eleventh century. In Kristin's time, however, the country's former paganism was not far beneath the surface of Christianity. At times of great distress, Kristin's contemporaries (and at least once Kristin herself) turn first to the Christian God, his Holy Mother, and the saints, and then, when all else fails, to the magic of the former pagan deities who were still thought to reside in forest glens and mountain halls. Only a few years after publishing the novel in 1920—to instant acclaim—Undset herself became a convert to the Roman faith.

What distinguishes Catholic Christianity from Protestant Christianity? If I may generalize: Catholicism is a faith of hermits and solitary pilgrims. The archetypal Catholic saint lies prostrate in silent solitude and candlelight before the crucifix, the symbol of a God-man who suffered and died alone. The Catholic drama of sin and salvation plays out in the privacy of one's own soul; every seeker walks alone through the valley of darkness, hoping to find the light. Catholicism remains today deeply medieval—even pagan—in its rites, arts, and institutions. Catholic liturgy is intimately connected to the annual and diurnal solar cycles (even more so when I was a child). The monastic cloister with its fixed round of prayer and rule of obedience to proper authority is the paradigm of Catholic faith. By contrast, Protestant Christianity is a faith of the new sixteenth-century

European middle-class. It is a religion of collective worship, of daylight and urban clatter, of the entrepreneurial spirit. The Protestant's journey toward salvation is played out in the marketplace; virtue and sin are a matter for God's ledger book. The paradigmatic virtues of Protestantism are thrift, industry, tidiness, and collective attention to numbered hymnals and the Book of Common Prayer. The only proper authority is God himself, as he speaks through scriptures.

So yes, *Kristin Lavransdatter* is a Catholic novel, as I am Catholic to the soles of my feet, although I have long since lapsed theologically from that faith (and every institutional faith) into a robust agnosticism. Never mind: I still walk the walk with Kristin. I share her love of the natural world, her sense that the world is shot through with powers we don't begin to understand. When Kristin struggles with her Latin prayers in a dark recess of the cathedral at Nidaros, barely knowing what the formulaic words signify, only that they are a kind of magical incantation, I am with her, because I know, as she knows, that for all the learning, honor, law, and material prosperity that make our lives tolerable, we live in a world that is deep beyond our knowing, and profoundly worthy of our reverence and awe.

And I will say this too, controversially I'm sure. Although everlasting life is an article of Catholic faith, immortality looms much less large in the Catholic sensibility than in Protestantism. We Catholics are dreadfully attached to *this* world of water, wax, bread and wine, flesh and blood, incense, chrism, light and darkness—in short, all those things the Reformists dismissed as idolatrous. We don't wait to be raptured out of our bodies; if we are going to some other place, we want to take our bodies with us. Hence the doctrine of the resurrection of the body; for the Catholic, everlasting life will only be tolerable if we can feel the thump of blood and the pangs of carnality. When Kristin dies, Ulf Haldorsson, a faithful friend who like so many other men loved her, regrets that he had not been more forthright in acting on his desire, even though to do so might have cost him his immortal soul. The priest Sira Eiliv says to him: "So it's futile to regret a good deed, Ulf, for the good you have done cannot be taken back; even if all the mountains should fall, it would still stand." And *that* is immortality enough for the Catholic.

So I share much with Kristin, by virtue of my early religious upbringing and education. But there is much that is different too between Kristin and me—not least of which is the security that has come with empirical science.

Kristin lived at a time when fifty was a fine old age. Death for mother or infant at childbirth was common; no modern woman would want to endure the agony that Kristin suffers with her first birthing. Vagaries of weather meant hunger or full bellies. A nick from a knife could mean sepsis and death. Men went about armed, and a fatal blow of an ax or sword might be occasioned by a minor slight. The Black Death, when it came, was an all-consuming holocaust. All of that has changed, at least for those of us fortunate enough to live in the secular, developed world. The Scientific Revolution and the Enlightenment left human nature intact, but they utterly transformed the material circumstances of our lives. Perhaps the most telling difference between Kristin's world and our own is this: for Kristin, every event is the handiwork of a personal God. Of the Black Death, she thinks: "This was the plague—God's punishment for the secret hardheartedness of every human being, which only God the Almighty could see." By contrast, we who embrace Enlightenment values believe that human nature has been shaped by billions of years of evolution, that we are each of us capable of virtue and evil, that physical and mental illness have natural causes, and that collectively and as individuals we are able to order our lives as we see fit. Nature might still sometimes smite us with apparently arbitrary tribulations—sickness, accident, storm, tidal wave, volcanic eruption—but innocence or guilt have nothing to do with it. No personal deity sits on high sending thunderbolts or blessings our way. If we choose to be good, we do so not because we anticipate everlasting bliss or fear hellfire, but because altruistic genes and common sense compel us to do so.

Blades play an important role in Undset's novel; a lot of bloody hacking goes on. But the blade that most forcefully separates the modern religious naturalist from Kristin's world is Ockham's razor. With it we have pared away a vast overlay of spirits and demons, elf maidens and mountain kings, miracles and supernatural manifestations of every sort. We have replaced those arbitrary forces with genes, germs, and natural law—and perhaps a dose of quantum indeterminacy—all very much a part of *this* world of beauty, mystery, joy, and sorrow. In such a world we make our pilgrimage out of darkness into such light as we can find, never forgetting that our faith—like Kristin's—must be judged ultimately not by pope, bishops, priests, or councils, not by holy books or ancient traditions, but by the greater happiness of humankind.

Near the beginning of the novel, a holy man, Brother Edvin, says to Kristin:

> There is no one, Kristin, who does not love and fear God. But it is because our hearts are divided between love for God and fear of the Devil, and love for this world and this flesh, that we are miserable in life and death. For if a man knew no yearning for God and God's being, then he would thrive in Hell, and we alone would not understand that he had found his heart's desire. Then the fire would not burn him if he did not long for coolness, and he would not feel the pain of the serpent's bite if he did not long for peace.

All of the material accouterments of modernity do not necessarily make us happier than people of Kristin Lavransdatter's time, but they do make it easier to live in this world and this flesh. What we share with Kristin and Brother Edvin is a longing, always, for coolness and peace.

Sigrid Undset's *Kristin Lavransdatter* won the Nobel Prize for literature in 1928. It would be difficult to summarize the subject of so sweeping a novel in a few words, but this would come close: The transforming power of the holy. The holy, for Undset, resides in individuals, not in nature, nor in institutions. It is the individual's capacity to love and suffer unselfishly—in spite of, or perhaps because of, his or her imperfections—that redeems a world broken by sin. Undset was raised an agnostic, but at the age of forty two she was received into the Roman Catholic Church. The first volume of *Kristen Lavransdatter* was published four years before her communion with the Church and foreshadows her conversion. It became part of that wonderful brew of Catholic literature—George Bernanos, Leon Bloy, Charles Péguy, Francois Mauriac, Graham Greene, and others—that fed the spirits of young Catholic intellectuals in the 1950s.

Another of Undset's books left its mark on some of us who came of age in the '50s: *Gunnar's Daughter*. A much shorter book, but no less impressive. The story is set around the year 1000 (four centuries before Kristin's time), as Christianity was just infiltrating the pagan north. In *Gunnar's Daughter* we witness the clash of two world views, the one grounded in flesh, blood, and iron, a polytheistic pagan faith of dark northern forests, the other a softer, more otherworldly Christian monotheism of the hot, sunny south.

Briefly, the story is this: The Icelander Ljot and the Norwegian maiden Vigdis meet as youths and fall in love. Tenderness is shattered when Ljot ravishes Vigdis in a fit of carnal passion. Their lives diverge but their fates are sealed. Vigdis cannot forgive Ljot's transgression and nurses a fierce hatred for him that springs from an equally fierce love betrayed. Ljot cannot forgive himself. Stubbornness and remorse turn what might have been a happy ending into unmitigated tragedy. Ljot and Vigdis were raised in a Viking culture in which the bravest and strongest are honored and the weak are expendable. Violated honor unleashes bloody cascades of revenge, sometimes spinning across many generations. Children are loved, but die with tragic regularity. Fidelity to kith and kin is visceral and tightly hemmed. Happiness is caught on the fly, when it can be caught at all.

Then comes Christianity with its instruction to turn the other cheek, to care for the weak, to love the stranger as one's self. Daily life is now structured by a rubric of feast, fasting, and prayer. For the first time, Norway is united under one king—the sainted Olav—and one law. Damaged or unwanted children are no longer exposed to die. Wives are no longer put away at will. Viking rapine and pillage are reserved for heathens and infidels. Vigdis embraces Christianity but the new religion makes her no happier than does Ljot's paganism, and Ljot's paganism makes him no less a good person than does Vigdis's Christianity. With the coming of the Christian faith, one set of intolerances is replaced by another. In both worlds—the pagan and the Christian—good and evil clash, and people struggle to find love and meet their material needs. In both worlds, the hidden holy occasionally blazes out with transforming power and effect.

For Undset, of course, the holy is a manifestation of God's providence, and Christian sanctity is a pearl beyond price. "All men more or less are moral cripples," she wrote in an essay. "But only when we are good in the way in which God is good, are we good enough." Undset writes within a Catholic context of Original Sin, from which we are saved by Christ's redemptive action—all of which is a theological way of explaining what we now at least partly understand through evolutionary biology. Non-human nature is red in tooth and claw, sometimes gruesomely so. Death is the evolutionary engine of complexification. Humans have inherited that propensity for violence, especially, it seems, through the male chromosome. But violence and "get mine" are not the only biological strategies for evolutionary success. It seems likely that we have also inherited altruistic genes that incline us towards the care of children, kin, and neighbors. We see these opposing innate behaviors—violence and altruism—powerfully at work in Undset's medieval novels.

Our behaviors are not only the product of biological evolution. Cultural evolution takes up where the genes leave off, and thus we have, for example, the teachings of the Buddha or of Christ. This conflict too—the Sermon on the Mount, say, versus the selfish gene—are at work in Undset's novels.

One need not accept Sigrid Undset's theology to learn important truths about human nature from her medieval tales. By taking us back to a time when love, family, childbirth, sexual passion, bloodlust, greed, and death were more starkly rendered by the mere struggle to survive, she forces us to reflect upon our own reasons for being faithful and good. We are *not* born moral cripples, as Undset supposes. We are born—as Ljot and Vigdis were born—with a mixed tangle of genetic predispositions. The great cultural project for people of good faith everywhere—theists, atheists, and religious naturalists—is to incline our biological proclivities toward the greatest good for all. That means first of all understanding our own passions—good and bad—and that is the reason I so often gave my students Undset's *Kristin Lavransdatter* as a graduation gift.

In an earlier chapter I quoted the physicist Heinz Pagels on the beginning of science:

> The capacity to tolerate complexity and welcome contradiction, not the need for simplicity and certainty, is the attribute of an explorer. Centuries ago, when some

people suspended their search for absolute truth and began instead to ask how things worked, modern science was born. Curiously, it was by abandoning the search for absolute truth that science began to make progress, opening the material universe to human exploration.

If one wanted to translate Pagels's remark into religious language, it would go something like this: the absence of God makes everything holy.

But why use religious language when Pagels's quite satisfactory summation says it all? Because for some of us—religious naturalists—Pagels's summation is incomplete. We are—for better or worse—religious by nature. Whether by genes or from thousands of years of encountering a deeply mysterious world in wakefulness and in dream, we have evolved a felt attraction to the trans-sensual. Any language that gives expression to our *trans-sensual* intuitions is religious. Let me say clearly: All personal gods are idolatrous, especially any personal god we dignify with a capital G. The great service to humanity of science has been to sweep the anthropomorphic gods away, or, at the very least, to show them for what they are, phantoms of the human brain. What we are given in their place is not Truth, but reliable empirical knowledge of the world, tentative and evolving. To be sure, science does not exhaust reality, or even begin to encompass the complexity of our interaction with the world. The religious naturalist seeks a language of spirituality that is consistent with the empirical way of knowing.

When the slate of religious superstition has been wiped clean, what are we left with? Silence? Yes, there is something to be said for silence, for retreating into what Thomas Merton called "the prayer of the heart." The Greek writer Nikos Kazantzakis in his *Spiritual Exercises* writes of the thing that he—hesitantly—calls Spirit:

> We struggle to make this Spirit visible, to give it a face, to encase it in words, in allegories and thoughts and

incantations, that it may not escape us. But it cannot be contained in the twenty-six letters of an alphabet which we string out in rows; we know that all these words, these allegories, these thoughts, and these incantations are, once more, but a new mask with which to conceal the Abyss.

Let it only be said that the world is shot through with a mystery that manifests itself no less in what is revealed by science—the universe of the galaxies and the eons, the eternally weaving DNA, the electrochemical flickering that is consciousness—than in the creations of novelists, poets, visual artists, and musicians. So we stumble forward, trying to avoid the dogmas of blind faith or scientism. We try to make ourselves worthy of a universe of which we are an infinitesimal part. We will not all agree on what worthiness consists of. For the religious naturalist, it is a mix of cautious skepticism and celebration.

chapter twelve

The Eternal Silence of Infinite Spaces

Nature loves to hide. And we are driven by nature and nurture to peel away her veils, to discover what is hidden. In doing so, we have had some surprises. Atoms. Germs. Genes. Galaxies. Electromagnetic radiation. Artificial intelligence. But also we discover that some things we long assumed to lie behind the goddess's veil have yielded scant evidence of their reality. Magic. Miracles. Gods and demons. Immortality.

Immortality. *Personal* immortality. Nothing has been more ardently wished for or universally believed. Nothing has so thoroughly covered its traces—if it exists. We have seen that every observable element of self is inextricably linked to matter. The conclusion seems inescapable. There is no ghost in the machine, no spirit that will survive the soma's death. This need not be a cause for dismay. The smallest insect is more worthy of our astonishment than a thousand choirs of angels. The buzzing business of a single cell is more infused with eternity than any disembodied soul.

Few poems of the previous century have attracted more discussion than Wallace Stevens's "Sunday Morning." In its ambivalence, its nostalgia for traditional faith, its frank hedonism, its skepticism, and its final, halting resolution, it captures as well as any other document our own *restlessness* in the face of death. Briefly, the poem describes a woman's thoughts and feelings as she sits in a sunny chair on a Sunday morning, indulging herself with coffee, oranges, and the "green freedom of a cockatoo." Into her dreamy reverie comes "the dark encroachment of that old catastrophe," Christ's bloody sacrifice, with its promise of her own resurrection into eternal life. But what would this promised paradise be with its ripe fruit that never falls, boughs that always hang heavy in a perfect sky? Where in that heavenly abode might she find the delight of hearing wakened birds test before they fly "the reality of misty fields, by their sweet questionings"? "Death is the mother of beauty," the poet writes, not once, but twice. Only in the face of personal oblivion do we attend to the sweet perfections of the here and now: "Passions of rain, or moods in falling snow; grievings in loneliness, or unsubdued elations when the forest blooms; gusty emotions on wet roads on autumn nights; all pleasures and all pains, remembering. . . ."

Why do we die? What is it about our biology that requires our inevitable, programmed death? Bacteria and amoebae reproduce by splitting down the middle, cloning themselves in a kind of immortality. An individual bacterium or amoeba might die—by being exposed to the excessive heat, for example—but it *need* not die. Its lineage can endure forever. Even sexual microorganisms, such as certain algae and fungi, can reproduce either sexually, jumbling genes, or by simple division, making millions of exact copies of themselves.

Death as we understand it entered the story with the advent of multicellularity. During the Cambrian Era, sexual creatures evolved made of two kinds of cells: germ cells— eggs and sperm—stored in the gonads and destined to play a role in reproduction, and soma cells—body cells—such as tissue, skeleton, stalk, stem, blood, heart, eyes, ears, horns, feathers. The germ cells have a kind of immortality in that their genome, or part of it, finds its way into future genera- tions. But the soma is doomed to die, perhaps in days, as for mayflies, or in centuries, as for sequoias.

It is the death of the soma that the woman in Stevens's poem is thinking about—the soma who sits in the sunny chair, wrapped in her silken dressing gown, inhaling the aroma of coffee, tasting the tangy fruit. The fact that some- thing of ourselves—the germ cells—can flow into future generations is little consolation for the death of the part of us that thinks, feels, dreams. The *soma* we see in the mirror is self-afflicted by thoughts of mortality. "But in content- ment I still feel the need of some imperishable bliss," says the woman in the poem, and, yes, a longing for immortality is deep within us, in our culture, perhaps even in our genes. To assuage the woman's unease, the poet offers no deathless paradise, only the enduring beauty of creation—the deer on the mountain, the sweet berries that ripen in the wilder- ness, the flocks of pigeons that in the evening make "ambiguous undulations as they sink, downward to dark- ness, on extended wings."

Will it be enough? Having stripped away death's veil and discovered no Empyrean Fields, no paradise, no spirit that can live forever, can the religious naturalist find sufficient consolation in the material creation? The microbiologist Ursula Goodenough writes: "Sex without death gets you single-celled algae and fungi; sex with a mortal soma gets you the rest of the . . . creatures. Death is the price paid to have trees and clams and birds and grasshoppers, and death is the price paid to have human consciousness, to be aware of all that shimmering awareness and all that love." Death, she might as well have said, is the mother of beauty.

On rare occasions the Leonid meteor shower of November puts on quite a show. Such was the case on the night of November 13–14, 1866, when the sky over Europe was literally ablaze with shooting stars. By all reports the spectacle was both terrifying and beautiful. It was, in any event, a sobering reminder of the precarious and imperson-al power of nature. A week or so after the shower, the English author and Anglican divine Charles Kingsley preached a sermon, which he titled "The Meteor Shower," which bears attention today. In that sermon he said:

> Terrible enough Nature looks to the savage, who thinks it crushes him from mere caprice. More terrible still does Science make Nature look, when she tells us that it crushes, not by caprice, but by brute necessity; not by ill-will, but by inevitable law. Science frees us in many ways (and all thanks to her) from the bodily terror which the savage feels. But she replaces that, in the minds of many, by a moral terror which is far more overwhelming.

The moral terror of which Charles Kingsley speaks is the *indifference* of the cosmos to our personal fates, exemplified most dramatically in our inevitable personal oblivion. Only faith in a higher guiding power can keep us from despair, preached Kingsley.

How I would love to see a meteor storm such as the one Kingsley observed in 1866. When several years ago a power-ful Leonid shower was predicted, you can bet I was out there waiting, only to be disappointed. I've seen some pret-ty good meteor showers, but nothing yet to equal the Leonids of 1866. We know exactly what causes these exceptional showers, and astronomers can predict them to some extent years in advance. No longer do we experience the raw terror that our ancestors felt on seeing the heavens fall. We appreciate meteor storms for what they are: demonstrations of nature's grandeur and beauty—and of the power of the human mind to grasp the laws that nature loves to hide.

In place of the distressingly indifferent laws of celestial mechanics, Kingsley—good Victorian divine—insinuates a Divine Father, outside of nature, loving to be sure, but also just, a Father who can suspend nature's laws to exact retribution, to punish the sinner, even to confine the unworthy to hell fire. Yes, science frees us in many ways from the physical terror which the "savage" feels, says Kingsley, and for that we should be grateful. Why then does he insist on returning us to a bondage of our own making? Is it necessary to feel the moral terror of hell to be good? Can we not find a basis for ethical action in joy, in beauty, in the gracious possibilities of human evolution? As a father, I want my children and grandchildren to be good not because they fear punishment or crave reward, but *because being good does honor to themselves and to the creation of which they are a part.* Call it grace if you wish. It is the same grace that illuminates the sky when meteors fly.

Several years ago, I attended a seminar at my college on the foundations of ethical systems. The participants, from various academic departments, quoted Plato, Jesus, Heidegger, and a host of other authorities; they trotted out every philosophical and theological reason why we can or should be good. Of course, prominent among the arguments was Kingsley's old canard: Without the promise of eternal salvation or the threat of damnation, we would all be scoundrels. No one at the seminar mentioned that we are first of all biological creatures with an evolutionary history, and that altruism, aggression, fidelity, promiscuity, nurturing, and violence might all be part of our animal natures. I

looked around the auditorium and saw folks of every religious and philosophical persuasion, and of many cultural
and ethnic backgrounds, and I thought, "Gee, I'd trust any
one of these folks to return my wallet if she found it lying in
the street." Sure, humans are capable of great evil, but most
of us are pretty good most of the time, and I suspect that it
has more to do with where we have been as a biological
species than with where we hope to be going in an afterlife.

   There have been many treatises in recent years showing
"how nature designed our universal sense of right and
wrong," to quote the subtitle of evolutionary psychologist
Marc Hauser's *Moral Minds*. Primatologists such as Dutch-
born Frans de Waal have described examples of empathetic
behavior among apes and monkeys; we are not, it seems,
the only moral animal. These studies are only a prologue to
what will be an ongoing investigation, and it is still too early
to offer firm conclusions, but few scientists doubt that
biological and cultural evolution can satisfactorily account
for moral behavior without invoking eternal punishments
or rewards.

   The debate about the foundations of morality was old
even in Kingsley's time. Some few decades after Kingsley
preached his Leonid sermon, the British statesman Arthur
Balfour addressed the problem of the good in a book called
The Foundations of Belief. Balfour compared what he imagined to be the God-given moral law to the starry heavens
and found them—as did Kingsley—both sublime. But if one
accepts the "naturalistic hypothesis," he wrote—thinking, of
course, of Darwin—then the moral law becomes as mundane as "the protective blotches on the beetle's back," an
ingenious contrivance of nature, perhaps, but hardly worthy
of our human affinity to angels. Balfour, like Kingsley, miss-
es the point. The Darwinian naturalistic synthesis does not
reduce the sublimity of the starry sky to the lowly beetle's
spots; rather *it shows the beetle's spots to be as sublime as any
starry sky*. Naturalism spins a web of enchantment that

equally embraces the beetle and the distant galaxy. No more do we think of nature as a "Great Chain of Being," with the moral law descending from above and the flames of hell licking our feet from below, as was the universal Christian belief before the Scientific Revolution. Since Galileo, we understand ourselves to be part of an endlessly fructifying tapestry of mutual relationship and self-imposed responsibility, rather than a chain of subservience and domination. We are animals who have evolved the capacity to cherish our fellow humans and to resist for the common good our innate tendencies to aggression and selfishness, not because we have been plucked out of our animal selves by some sky hook from above, but because we have been nudged into reflective consciousness by evolution. When it comes to living in a civilized way on a crowded planet, I choose to put my faith in the long leash of the genes rather than fear of hellfire or a chance to walk on streets of gold.

In the first panel of a Calvin and Hobbes comic strip, Calvin is alone under the night sky. In the second panel, he screams at the stars, *"I'm significant!"* Third panel: He stands staring into the silent spaces. Fourth panel: A chastened Calvin adds, "Screamed the dust speck."

Auggghhhhhh. . . ! Poor Calvin. Overwhelmed with the vastness of the cosmos and existential angst. He is not the first, of course. Most famously the seventeenth-century French philosopher Blaise Pascal wailed his own despair: "I feel engulfed in the infinite immensity of spaces whereof I know nothing and which know nothing of me. I am terrified. . . . The eternal silence of these infinite spaces alarms me."

And he didn't know the half of it.

Not so long ago, we imagined ourselves to be the be-all and end-all of creation, at the center of a cosmos made expressly for us. We stood at the pinnacle of the material Great Chain of Being, just a step below the spiritual angels.

We could almost touch the hem of God's robe as he sat on his celestial throne in the all-enclosing Empyrean sphere. Then it turned out with Copernicus that the Earth is not the center of the cosmos. Nor, we subsequently discovered, is the Sun. Nor the Galaxy. The astronomers Sebastian von Hoerner and Carl Sagan raised this apparently deflating experience to the level of a principle—the Principle of Mediocrity, they called it—which can be stated like this: *The view from here is about the same as the view from anywhere else.* Or to put it another way: Our star, our planet, the life on it, and even our own intelligence, are completely mediocre. Moon rocks are just like Earth rocks. Photographs of the surface of Mars made by the landers and rovers might as well have been made in Nevada. Meteorites contain some of the same organic compounds that are the basis for terrestrial life. Gas clouds in the space between the stars are composed of precisely the same atoms and molecules that we find in our own backyard. The most distant galaxies betray in their spectra the presence of familiar elements.

And yet, and yet, for all we know, our brains are the most complex things in the universe. It could be, I suppose, that we are living, breathing refutations of the Principle of Mediocrity, utterly unique with our intelligence and self-awareness among the myriad galaxies. But I doubt it. For the time being, Calvin will just have to get used to living in the infinite abyss and eternal silence. He has Hobbes, his beloved tiger. We have each other.

I think of something the Jesuit mystic Pierre Teilhard de Chardin wrote, something similar to Calvin's scream: "It is a terrifying thing to have been born: I mean, to find one's self, without having willed it, swept irrevocably along on a torrent of fearful energy." But Teilhard, recognizing the Pascalean silences of space, found the grounds for exhilaration in the great sweep of natural evolution, and identified his God with "the flame [that] has lit up the whole world from within . . . from the inmost core of the tiniest atom to the mighty sweep of the most universal laws of being." He wrote: "Man has every right to be anxious of his fate so long as he feels himself to be lost and lonely in the midst of the mass of created things. But let him once discover that his fate is bound up with the fate of nature itself, and immediately, joyously, he will begin again his forward march." Teilhard turned the terror of infinite spaces into an overwhelming joy. He died, in exile, with much of his life's work censored by the Church to which he had dedicated his life, a Church that meant to keep for itself the keys to the gates of heaven and the doors of hell, a Church that had a vested interest in maintaining the illusion of a personal God to whom she controls exclusive access. That was surely a great trial for Teilhard. But his greatest sadness at the end was this: "How is it possible that I am so incapable of passing on to others . . . the vision of the marvelous unity in which I find myself immersed."

Recently, I watched again, for the first time since the late 1950s, Robert Bresson's classic film, *The Diary of a Country Priest*, based on Georges Bernanos's novel of the same name. I am reminded of the film now as I write of Teilhard de Chardin's death in exile from his beloved France and the favor of his Church. The story is that of a young priest who arrives at his first parish in rural France filled with naive idealism, spiritual longing, and a good bit of repressed sexuality. He lives in a world haunted by God and demons. Spurned by his parishioners, unable to pray, his stomach ravaged by cancer, the young priest drifts inexorably towards death. His last words are: "Does it matter? Grace is everywhere. . . ."

Both film and book made a great impression on me when I encountered them half-a-century ago. I was then a young graduate student in physics, deeply religious, struggling to find my way between faith-based reality and evidence-based reality. After some years of anguished searching (and no small amount of stomach pain), I chose empiricism over faith. Does it matter? Oh yes. I have lived the greater part of my life without God or demons, and I am happily rewarded for it. I have come to the same conclusion as Teilhard de Chardin and Georges Bernanos's country priest: Grace is everywhere.

chapter thirteen

The
Modesty
of Truth

S o there she stands on a pedestal in the Musee d'Orsay
in Paris, Louis Barrias's *Nature Unveiling Herself to
Science*, created by the sculptor in 1899, the veiled
goddess Isis, one of humankind's most enduring metaphors
for the mystery that confronts us on every side. *Nature loves
to hide,* said Heraclitus more than two thousand years ago.
"It is the glory of God to conceal a thing, and the honor of
kings to search it out," agreed the great Russian chemist
Dmitri Mendeleev, giving voice to the motivation of scientists everywhere.

The metaphor of veiled Isis—Mother Nature—is as old as
our quest for understanding of the world. Bite the apple
from the Tree of Knowledge. Open Pandora's box. Lift
the goddess's veil. Will what we find make us the equal of

the gods? Or will our hubris bring us low? Should we leave
the goddess's veil intact, as the Romantic poets insist? In
Friedrich Schiller's poem "The Veiled Statue [of Isis] at Sais,"
a youth, having been warned that the veil is light to the
touch but heavy with consequence, nevertheless slips into
the goddess's temple at night and, cautiously, terrified, rais-
es the concealing cloth. He is struck senseless, reduced to
melancholy—the story of Adam and Eve and the Tree of
Knowledge all over again. Even the occasional scientist hes-
itates as he approaches the goddess. The DNA researcher
Erwin Chargaff opined: "Scientific curiosity is not an
unbounded good. . . . Restraint in asking necessary questions is one of the sacrifices that even the scientist ought to
be willing to make to human dignity."

Most people choose to ignore the goddess and her veils;
they believe that holy books, shamans, prophets, or preachers
have told them all they need to know. Some of us, however—
call us agnostics, or better, religious naturalists—walk a path
somewhere between the questing confidence of a Mendeleev
and the restraint of a Schiller—between boldly approaching
the goddess and stripping off her veils, or being content that
some part of her should stay wrapped in mystery.

Among the ancients, Mother Nature was more than a
metaphor. The veiled goddess was invented at a time when
animism and anthropomorphism were the prevailing ways
of understanding the world. Every brook, every stone, every
heavenly body was thought to have a human-like spirit. The
gods themselves were humans writ large. Barrias's *Isis* in
the Musee d'Orsay is herself endearingly human; look!
beneath the veil, the bared breasts, the white flesh. With
such a representation of Nature it was altogether reasonable
to imagine that it might be possible—for good or ill—to strip
nature bare.

But we no longer understand nature animistically or
anthropomorphically. New metaphors now instruct our
imaginations. If one reads the weekly issues of *Science* and

Nature, for example, the two most prominent science journals, it is the metaphor of *nature as a machine* that one encounters almost exclusively. Here are a few terms from a recent issue: *cellular machinery, molecular machines, molecular motors, replication mechanisms, mechanisms for maintenance of DNA integrity.* The mechanical metaphor has been the basis of scientific thought since the seventeenth century, when a scientific revolution coincided (not coincidentally) with a time of mechanical innovation. The metaphor has been spectacularly fruitful, and has some life in it yet; at least, no more useful metaphor has come along. But the mechanical metaphor has recently taken on a new twist: the seventeenth-century clockwork of gears and levers is giving way to the electronic chip—nature as hardware and software. Here is how the geneticist Enrico Coen describes life in his book, *The Art of Genes*: "The software, the program [DNA], is responsible for organizing hardware, the organism. Yet throughout the process, it is the organism in its various stages of development that has to run the program." In other words, in Coen's analogy, the hardware runs the software, while at the same time the software is generating the hardware. A computer is a machine, yes, but a rather different sort of machine than the clockwork.

Keep two things in mind. First, "life is a machine" or "life is a computer" are only metaphors. All understanding is metaphorical—in science, in poetry, even in theology. Few people any longer mistake the gray-bearded man on the ceiling of the Sistine Chapel for the Creator of the universe, but Michelangelo's metaphor still powerfully resonates with those who believe in a personal God. Second, the mechanical metaphor for life does not so much reduce the marvelous to the mundane, as it elevates the mundane to the marvelous. "Mundane" comes from the Latin *mundus*, meaning "world." The more we understand the staggeringly complex molecular machinery of life, the more truly marvelous the world becomes.

But I've been told more times than I can count: Think of life as a machine and you'll treat life as a machine. As I write, I am again watching a hummingbird at the feeder outside my window and I hear the scolding voices: Think of the hummingbird as a little whirring clockwork, and you'll treat it as a clockwork. Well, no. I don't treat the hummingbird as a clockwork. But what makes the hummingbird different is not that the bird has an irreducible hummingbird soul, but complexity. Even a single cell in the hummingbird's body is vastly more complex than the most elaborate clockwork. It is the *overwhelming complexity* of the hummingbird that commands my reverence and my love. And my appreciation for the hummingbird is enhanced by everything I know biologically about its metabolism, its aerodynamics, its biochemistry—in short, everything we have learned by application of the mechanical metaphor. The idea of an irreducible, incorporeal soul is lovely, but it has led exactly nowhere. And before you say "So what?" ask yourself if you would prefer to live in a world without modern medicine. If your child had polio or bird flu, would you rather know about mechanically-reducible viral biochemistry or irreducible souls? If you answer the latter, then at least you are consistent in rejecting the mechanical metaphor for life.

With new metaphors (and the corresponding new instruments) science has revealed to our astonished eyes the universe of the galaxies and the quarks, neuronal nets and DNA—a universe that cannot be remotely comprehended with animistic and anthropomorphic metaphors. And the corollary of these remarkable discoveries is profound. Yes, our knowledge has increased dramatically, but so has our awareness of what we do not know. This is perhaps the most important *scientific* discovery of the last century: our ignorance. *Nature loves to hide.* Perhaps her ultimate secrets are hidden forever. Our minds, after all, are finite; the universe may be infinite. We lift the veil, we find another. And another. And another. And we are back where we began with Heraclitus.

The astonishing success of the mechanical metaphor has led not to hubris but to humility—a profound awareness of what we do not know. Make no mistake: The mechanical metaphor does not exhaust the world's meaning. For the religious naturalist, the universe sings beyond any metaphor we employ to understand it. We are enchanted by the veiled goddess, teased, seduced. We lift her veils in a kind of unending foreplay. We expect no consummation. We would in fact be rather shattered if somehow we were allowed to know the ultimate secrets of the universe.

The coy goddess conceals her secrets in the humming-bird's electric heart and in the new-borning stars of the Great Orion Nebula, in the spinning molecular motors of DNA and in the flower in the crannied wall. No, not hubris, but humility. Not self-certainty, but the modesty of truth with a lowercase *t*. Our knowledge is finite, our ignorance infinite.

We will have no beatific vision in this world or any other. In compensation, I take from my Catholic upbringing a sacramental view of the world. In Catholic theology, a sacrament is an outward sign of invisible grace, instituted by God for our sanctification. Here is a paragraph from the on-line Catholic Encyclopedia:

> The reasons underlying a sacramental system are as follows: Taking the word "sacrament" in its broadest sense, as the sign of something sacred and hidden (the Greek word is "mystery"), we can say that the whole world is a vast sacramental system, in that material things are unto men the signs of things spiritual and sacred, even of the Divinity.

It's a simple and elegant formulation that survives translation into the language of the scientific agnostic: Every object of the natural world bears within itself a mostly hidden relationship to every other object. In attending prayerfully to these webs of relationship we integrate ourselves more fully into the fabric of the universe. Grace, in this sense, is that which enables us to live gracefully.

And grace—as Bernanos's country priest said—is everywhere. When God is gone, everything is holy. "Praise *this* world to the Angel," says the poet Rainer Maria Rilke. "Do not tell him the untellable. . . . Show him some simple thing, refashioned by age after age, till it lives in our hands and eyes as a part of ourselves. Tell him *things*. He'll stand more astonished."

chapter one

"*. . . gave me a copy of Myles Connolly's novella. . . .*" I read Myles Connolly's *Mr. Blue* in the 1928 first edition, now long out of print. I am pleased to see that the book is available again, from Loyola Press, 2005, in the Loyola Classics series.

chapter two

"*His biographer. . . .*" Robert Bernard Martin, *Gerard Manley Hopkins: A Very Private Life*, New York: Putnam, 1991.

"*. . . manifest in his poetry. . . .*" The quotes from the poetry of Hopkins are from *The Poetical Works of Gerard Manley Hopkins,* ed. by Norman H. Mackenzie, Clarendon Press, Oxford, 1992. "As kingfishers catch fire. . . .", p. 141; "The world is charged. . . .", p. 139; "I am like a slip of comet. . . .", p. 40; "Cloud-puffball. . . .", p. 197.

"*I am sensual in order to be spiritual. . . .*" Mary Oliver, *Winter Hours,* Boston: 1999, Houghton Mifflin, p. 100.

"*We know from his writings. . . .*" For Hopkins on the night sky, I have relied on the astronomer David Levy's delightful *More Things in Heaven and Earth: Poets and Astronomers Read the Night Sky*, Wombat Press, Wolfville, Nova Scotia, 1997. A later revised edition is titled *Starry Night: Poets and Astronomers Read the Sky*, Prometheus Books, 2001.

chapter three

"I don't know exactly what a prayer is. . . ." "The Summer Day," Mary Oliver, *New and Selected Poems*, Boston: Beacon Press, 1992.

"In his Spiritual Exercises. . . ." Nikos Kazantzakis, The Saviors of God: Spiritual Exercises, Simon and Schuster, New York, 1960, is not nearly as well known as it should be.

"In the beginning. . . ." Teilhard de Chardin, "The Mass on the World", in *Hymn of the Universe*, New York: Harper and Row, 1961, p. 21.

"In his famous review. . . ." Peter Medawar, *Mind*, vol. 70, no. 277, January 1961, pp. 99–105.

chapter four

"His biographers. . . ." Adrian Desmond and James Moore, *Darwin: The Life of a Tormented Evolutionist,* Warner Books, 1992, p. 524.

"In a letter to the American biologist. . . ." Darwin's letter to Asa Gray, May 22, 1860, from *The Life and Letters of Charles Darwin,* ed. by Francis Darwin, New York: Basic Books, 1959, p. 105.

"The physicist Heinz Pagels. . . ." Heinz Pagels, *Perfect Symmetry,* New York: Simon and Schuster, 1985, p. 28.

"One entry I have always liked. . . ." Blaise Pascal, *Pensées,* V:327, Modern Library edition, New York: 1941, p. 110.

"The twentieth-century philosopher. . . ." Karl Popper, *Conjectures and Refutations,* New York: Basic Books, 1968, p. 28.

"The physician/essayist Lewis Thomas. . . ." Lewis Thomas, "Debating the Unknowable," *Atlantic Monthly,* July 1981, quoted by Timothy Ferris in *Coming of Age In the Milky Way,* New York: William Morrow, 1988, p. 383.

". . . the eighteenth-century English scientist. . . ." Joseph Priestley, *Experiments and Observations Relating to Various Branches of Natural Philosophy,* London: Pearson and Rollason, 1781, vol. 2, p. ix.

"In a 1931 letter to his sister. . . ." George Gaylord Simpson, *Simple Curiosity,* Berkeley: University of California, 1987, p. 156.

"When I reached intellectual maturity. . . ." The quote from Thomas Huxley is from his 1889 essay "Agnosticism." It is readily available on the web.

chapter five

". . . in words shuddering with indignation. . . ." Erwin Chargaff, "Engineering a Molecular Nightmare", *Nature,* vol. 327, no. 6119, May 21, 1987, p. 199.

"In his seminal study. . . ." Richard Foster Jones, *Ancients and Moderns: A Study of the Rise of the Scientific Movement in Seventeenth-century England,* St. Louis: Washington University, 1961, p. 119.

". . . the late great biologist Stephen Jay Gould. . . ." Michael Shermer, *Why People Believe Weird Things,* New York: W. H. Freeman, 1997, p. x.

". . . the Indian philosopher Meera Nanda." Meera Nanda, *Prophets Facing Backward: Postmodern Critiques of Science and Hindu Nationalism in India,* New Jersey: Rutgers University Press, 2004.

chapter six

"Larry Dossey is among the bestselling. . . ." Larry Dossey, *Healing Words,* New York: HarperOne, 1995.

". . . examined the 131 laboratory experiments. . . ." Robert Baker's critique of Dossey can be found on the web at www.csi-cop.org/sb/9409/skeptic.html and www.csicop.org/sb/9709/baker.html.

". . . Adrian van Maanen on the rotation of galaxies." The story of Adriaan van Maanen's work on galaxies is told in Richard Berendzen, Richard Hart and Daniel Seeley, *Man Discovers the Galaxies,* New York: Science History Publications, 1976.

chapter seven

"The description that follows is drawn. . . ." Grace Goldin, *Works of Mercy: A Picture History of Hospitals,* Ontario: Canada, Boston Mills Press, 1994.

"When I am liberated. . . ." Thomas Merton, *Thoughts in Solitude*, Farrar, New York: Straus and Cudahy, 1958, pp. 93–94.

"so much depends. . . ." William Carlos Williams, from *Collected Poems: 1909-1939*, vol. 1, 1938, New Directions Publishing Corp. Reprinted by permission of New Directions Publishing Corp.

chapter eight

". . . Head, neck, hair, ears. . . ." Walt Whitman, *Leaves of Grass*, New York: Modern Library, 1921, pp. 87–88.

". . . the surgeon Richard Selzer tells us. . . ." Richard Selzer, *Mortal Lessons: Notes on the Art of Surgery*, New York: Simon and Schuster, 1976, p. 15.

chapter nine

"He spells out his ideas. . . ." Dean Hamer, *The God Gene: How Faith Is Hardwired into Our Genes*, New York: Doubleday, 2004.

"Wilson writes. . . ." E. O. Wilson, *On Human Nature*, Cambridge, MA: Harvard University Press, 1979, p. 169.

"In the Varieties of Religious Experience. . . ." William James, *The Varieties of Religious Experience*, New York: Modern Library, 1994, p. 85.

"Almost a century later. . . ." E. O. Wilson, *Consilience: The Unity of Knowledge*, New York: Knopf, 1998, p. 261.

"In her wonderful book. . . ." Ursula Goodenough, *The Sacred Depths of Nature*, USA: Oxford University Press, 1998, p. 73.

". . . urges us to assimilate. . . ." Thomas Berry, "The New Story: Comments On the Origin, Identification and Transmission of Values," *Teilhard Studies*, vol. 1, winter 1978.

chapter ten

"Richard Dawkins's The God Delusion. . . ." Richard Dawkins, *The God Delusion*, Boston: Houghton Mifflin, 2006.

". . . and Sam Harris's The End of Faith." Sam Harris, *The End of Faith*, New York: W. W. Norton and Company, 2004.

". . . Matthew Fox's account of Eckhart's theology. . . ." My discussion of Eckhart draws upon Matthew Fox, *Breakthrough: Meister Eckhart's Creation Spirituality in New Translation,* Doubleday, 1980.

chapter eleven

"God, I have sought you. . . ." Alden Nowlan, "Sacrament," reprinted by permission of the poet's estate.

"Ursula Goodenough writes. . . ." Ursula Goodenough, *The Sacred Depths of Nature,* Oxford University Press, USA, 1998, p. 30.

"Listen again to the Roman Catholic priest. . . ." From Thomas Berry's introduction to Thomas Merton, *When the Trees Say Nothing: Writings on Nature,* Notre Dame, IN: Sorin Books, 2003, p. 17–18.

"The book I gave most often. . . ." Sigrid Undset, *Kristin Lavransdatter,* translated by Tina Nunnally, New York: Penguin Classics, 2005.

"Another of Undset's books. . . ." Sigrid Undset, *Gunnar's Daughter,* translated by Arthur Chater, New York: Penguin Classics, 1998.

"The Greek writer Nikos Kazantzakis. . . ." Nikos Kazantzakis, *The Saviors of God: Spiritual Exercises,* New York: Simon and Schuster, 1960, p. 100.

chapter twelve

"The microbiologist Ursula Goodenough writes. . . ." Ursula Goodenough, *The Sacred Depths of Nature,* USA: Oxford University Press, 1998, p. 151.

"In that sermon he said. . . ." Charles Kingsley's sermon "The Meteor Shower" is readily available on the web.

"Arthur Balfour addressed the problem. . . ." Arthur Balfour, *The Foundations of Belief,* New York and London: Longmans Green and Company, 1895.

"It is a terrifying thing to have been born. . . ." Teilhard de Chardin, *Hymn of the Universe,* New York: Harper and Row, 1961, pp. 23, 29, 107.

"... *based on Georges Bernanos's novel.* ..." Georges Bernanos, *Diary of a Country Priest,* New York: Carroll and Graf, 2002.

chapter thirteen

"*Here is how the geneticist.* ..." Enrico Coen, *The Art of Genes,* Oxford: Oxford University, 1999, p. 11.

DEC X   2008